Timeless Truths Priceless Promises

Timeless Truths Priceless Promises

Compiled by
LINDA GRAMATKY SMITH

Grason
Box 1240
Minneapolis, MN 55440

WITH THANKS

Several people have contributed their talents to this book. I would like to send a special thank-you to Ronnie Gorini, a friend who provided help with editing, typing, insight and caring; to Sal Lazzarotti for creatively designing the book; and to Tu Bich for the care he gave to the book layout.

Unless otherwise noted, Scripture references herein are from the King James version of the Bible. Verses so indicated are taken from the *Living Bible*, ©1971 Tyndale House Publishers, Wheaton, Illinois. All rights reserved. Scripture identified RSV is from the Revised Standard Version of the Bible, copyrighted 1946, 1952, 1971 and 1973.

PHOTO CREDITS

Janet Shaffer, pgs. 1, 69, 103, 137, 138, 171.
Sal Lazzarotti, cover, pgs. 2, 35, 36, 104.
Will McIntyre, pgs. 70, 172.

Introduction

So often, as I was gathering the writings in this book, I thought back to the time a couple of years ago when my father was dying of cancer, a period of great sadness in my life. Some days I would be marveling over some shared story, some expression of love, some affirmation of the life we'd shared together; other days I would be traveling down the highway—with tears pouring down my cheeks saying, "But, Lord, he's my *Dad!*", not willing to have him leave the earth.

Most readers will understand the dichotomy I felt. In the lives of all of us there come times of discouragement and heartbreak when we feel that our mental, physical or spiritual bank accounts are overdrawn. At such times we may pray words similar to David's in Psalm 25:17—"The troubles of my heart are enlarged: O bring thou me out of my distress."

One way God has of bringing us out of our distress is to instruct us through the writings of His followers. Some people have claimed that a strong faith in Jesus Christ is all that is needed to avoid any pain and suffering, that by trusting in Him we can build an impenetrable shield that will deflect all problems; but the wise writers in this book reveal that even though we cannot avoid life's difficulties we can find a faith that helps us deal with them.

First of all, we have God's Holy Spirit to comfort and guide us. Then we have His Word to instruct and inspire us. And lastly, we have the witness of men and women of faith. Sometimes this witness comes from your backyard neighbor; sometimes it comes from the words and writings of spiritual giants who have shared their inspiration over the years.

In *Timeless Truths, Priceless Promises,* we have collected what we believe to be some of the greatest words of faith ever recorded. Some come from the greatest book of all, the Bible; others come from people who have dedicated their lives to serving God. Included are favorite hymns, moving stories, memorable poems, challenging sermons. Contributors represent a wide spectrum of Christians. Some are voices out of the distant past; others are contemporary followers of Jesus whose words have inspired all who seek the Kingdom of God. The writers have this in common: they speak with love and with a belief in the power of God.

We hope you'll be able to easily find help when you have a specific need. The selections have been gathered into twelve chapters according to the most common concerns and difficulties—loneliness, grief, worry, illness, confusion or doubt, for example. In addition, the index in the back will help you locate favorite authors.

My hope and prayer is that you will find *Timeless Truths, Priceless Promises* a helpful book, one to which you return again and again for spiritual enrichment, reassurance and inspiration.

Linda Gramatky Smith

Contents

1.

When Friends or Loved Ones Have Let You Down

There are many times in the lives of all of us when we feel unloved and unappreciated. And sometimes there seems to be no one to whom we can turn, no one with whom we can share the depth of hurt that we feel.

In such "dark nights of the soul," it is good to remember that the Lord always is ready to lend a sympathetic ear. He understands what it means to be deserted by friends and loved ones because during his life on earth he experienced the

sting of rejection often. Think of the pain Jesus must have felt in the Garden of Gethsemane. He had told his disciples Peter, James and John, "My soul is crushed by sorrow to the point of death; stay here and watch with me" (Mark 14 :34, Living Bible). But they let him down: when He returned, they were sleeping. The depth of His anguish is reflected in His words to Peter. "Simon!" he said. "Asleep? Couldn't you watch with me even one hour?"

Though friends may desert us, it is reassuring to know that Christ will not, that He will be with us in our hour of need whenever it comes. We have His unconditional word in Hebrews 13 :5—"I will never leave thee nor forsake thee." Remember His promise when the world lets you down.

Love ever gives—
Forgives—outlives—
And ever stands
With open hands.
And while it lives,
It gives.
For this is Love's prerogative—
To give, and give, and give.

John Oxenham

The Lord seeth not as man seeth, for man looketh on outward appearances, but the Lord looketh on the heart.

I Samuel 16 :7

Life is a mirror for king and for slave,
'Tis just what you are and do,
So give to the world the best you have,
And the best will come back to you.

Anonymous

We shall never agree on every issue but we can admit that the other fellow has a right to his opinions, and even though we differ, we do not need to hate. We are all human. As Alexander Pope said, 'To err is human; to forgive divine.' Disagreements can and often do turn into hatreds; they breed fights and fatal dissensions in the Church, and I hate *that* ... Love is the answer—godly, unselfish love for one's neighbor. Love is of no one color; it's made up of all colors. Since we were all created in His image and in His love, can we do less than love all His creatures?

Dale Evans Rogers

If God be for us, who can be against us?

Romans 8 :31

Never does the human soul appear so strong as when it forgoes revenge, and dares forgive an injury.

Edwin H. Chapin

In the weary,
waiting,
silence
of the night,
speak to me, Lord!

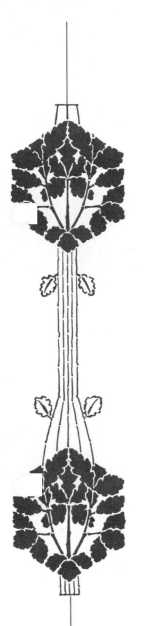

The others do—
haunting,
accusing,
foreboding;
the body tosses
and
the heart grows tight,
and
sleep, elusive, fades into
the
weary
waiting,
silence
of the night.

He speaks:
the mind,
preoccupied with sleeplessness,
is deaf.
Silently
He wraps me in His love;
so loved,
I rest.

Ruth Bell Graham

Life seems to me too short to be spent in nursing animosity or registering wrong.

Charlotte Brönte

If I had the gift of being able to speak in other languages without learning them, and could speak in every language there is in all of heaven and earth, but didn't love others, I would only be making noise. If I had the gift of prophecy and knew all about what is going to happen in the future, knew everything about *everything*, but didn't love others, what good would it do? Even if I had the gift of faith so that I could speak to a mountain and make it move, I would still be worth nothing at all without love. If I gave everything I have to poor people, and if I were burned alive for preaching the Gospel but didn't love others, it would be of no value whatever.

Love is very patient and kind, never jealous or envious, never boastful or proud, never haughty or selfish or rude. Love does not demand its own way. It is not irritable or touchy. It does not hold grudges and will hardly even notice when others do it wrong. It is never glad about injustice, but rejoices whenever truth wins out. If you love someone you will be loyal to him no matter what the cost. You will always believe in him, always expect the best of him, and always stand your ground in defending him.

All the special gifts and powers from God will someday come to an end, but love goes on forever. Someday prophecy, and speaking in unknown languages, and special knowledge — these gifts will disappear. Now we know so little, even with our special gifts, and the preaching of those most gifted is still so poor. But when we have been made perfect and complete, then the need for these inadequate special gifts will come to an end, and they will disappear.

It's like this: when I was a child I spoke and thought and reasoned as a child does. But when I became a man my thoughts grew far beyond those of my childhood, and now I have put away the childish things. In the same way, we can see and understand only a little about God now, as if we were peering at his reflection in a poor mirror; but someday we are going to see him in his completeness, face to face. Now all that I know is hazy and blurred, but then I will see everything clearly, just as clearly as God sees into my heart right now.

There are three things that remain—faith, hope and love— and the greatest of these is love.

I Corinthians 13 (Living Bible)

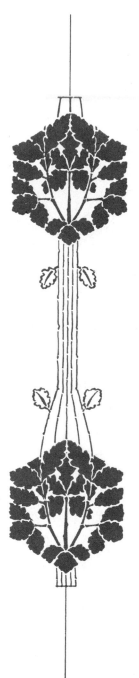

Lord, make me an instrument of Your peace.
Where there is hatred, let me sow love;
Where there is injury, pardon;
Where there is doubt, faith;
Where there is despair, hope;
Where there is darkness, light;
And where there is sadness, joy.

O Divine Master, grant that I may not
So much seek to be consoled as to console;
To be understood as to understand;
To be loved as to love;
For it is in giving that we receive;
It is in pardoning that we are pardoned;
And it is in dying
That we are born to eternal life.

Saint Francis of Assisi

His heart was as great as the world, but there was no room
in it to hold the memory of a wrong.

Ralph Waldo Emerson

Be not overcome of evil, but overcome evil with good.

Romans 12 :21

Let me be a little kinder,
Let me be a little blinder
To the faults of those around me,
Let me praise a little more.

Edgar Guest

Abide with me—fast falls the eventide;
The darkness deepens—Lord, with me abide;
When other helpers fail and comforts flee,
Help of the helpless, O abide with me.

Swift to its close ebbs out life's little day;
Earth's joys grow dim, its glories pass away;
Change and decay in all around I see;
O Thou who changest not, abide with me.

I fear no foe, with Thee at hand to bless;
Ills have no weight and tears no bitterness;
Where is death's sting? where, grave, thy victory?
I triumph still if Thou abide with me.

Henry F. Lyte (hymn)

Let not the sun go down upon your wrath.

Ephesians 4:26

Probably one of the forms of persecution which hurts us most is that of rejection. Basically, we all want to be accepted and loved. Instead, we may find ourselves spurned and cast off. Jesus Himself is the supreme example of experiencing rejection. "He was despised and rejected by men" (Isaiah 53:3). "He came to that which was his own but his own did not receive him." (John 1:11)

Billy Graham

Hatred toward any human being cannot exist in the same heart as love to God.

Dean Inge

He drew a circle that shut me out,
Heretic, rebel, a thing to flout.
But love and I had the wit to win;
We drew a circle that took him in.

Edwin Markham

While visiting a prison in Africa, I heard about a young man who was sentenced to die, and I asked to see him. The cell had a very high ceiling and one small window at the top for light. It was bare, except for a shelf very low to the ground. Sitting on that shelf was a handsome black African who had one more week to live. I was praying very hard! ... As we talked, I learned that the young man's name was Kimio and that he had a wife and children. Kimio knew about the Cross, and that Jesus had died there for the sins of the whole world.

I asked him if he knew who was responsible for his arrest and imprisonment. He was a political prisoner, and there came into his eyes the darkness of hatred.

"I can name every person responsible for my being here," he said.

"Can you forgive them?"

"No, I can't."

"I understand that. Once a man betrayed me and my whole family. Because of his betrayal, four of my family died in prison, and I suffered in three of the most horrible prisons in the whole world. And, Kimio, I could forgive that man. Not through my own strength—never—but through the Lord. The Holy Spirit can fill your heart with God's love, and He can give you the power to forgive. Kimio, I felt so free after I had forgiven that man. You have to die very soon."

"Yes, and I have a wife and children that I will never see again because of those men."

"I understand, Kimio, but you have to come before God. Jesus said, 'If you do not forgive those who wrong you, my

Heavenly Father will not forgive you.' So, Kimio, you *have* to forgive.''

We prayed and there was the presence of angels in that cell. Later I learned that Kimio wrote to his wife: "Love the people who have brought me here. Forgive them. You can't, and I can't, but Jesus *in* us is able.'' Kimio was trapped by the misery of this world, but he learned how to be free.

Corrie ten Boom

Never answer an angry word with
an angry word. It is the second one
that leads to a fight.

Author Unknown

A MOTHER SPEAKS

It is not gratitude, my child, I ask,
    Nor do I seek to make my will your own;
The memory of your babyhood, though you are grown
    Enchants me still; nor ever was a task
Performed for you save lovingly; I do
    Indeed thank you that you have brought me days
Of bright felicity in all your ways,
    And hours of grieving and of tears, so few!

No, do not thank me now, but think upon
    Your childhood tenderly when I have gone,
And if in sudden sweet remembering,
    You, too, find deepening joy in each small thing
Done for your child, or in your ministry
    To one beloved, you will be thanking me.

Anonymous

Forebearing one another, and forgiving one another...
as Christ forgave you, so also do ye.

Colossians 3 :13

Let there be no strife, I pray thee, between me and thee;
for we be brethren.

Genesis 13 :8

where people are, needs are hurts,
  searching, hunger.
if Jesus is in me, He can reach out to them.
on a plane, at a bus stop, in a restaurant at the
  shop or school.
He reaches out in things we do.
sir, my seat?
ma'am, take my hand.
did you need a dime?
can i help you with that?
tell me how you feel. i'll listen.
love makes the difference.

Ann Kiemel

What doth the Lord require of thee, but to do justly, and to love
mercy, and to walk humbly with thy God?

Micah 6 :8

The measure of a Christian is not in the height of his grasp,
but in the depth of his love.

Clarence Jordan

Full many a gem of purest ray serene
The dark unfathom'd caves of ocean bear:
Full many a flower is born to blush unseen,
And waste its sweetness on the desert air.

Thomas Gray

When I walked through death's dark valley,
    I was broken with woe,
All my friends seemed to forsake me,
    and I knew not where to go.
Then I heard the Saviour calling,
    midst the darkness and the din,
And he whispered, "I'll be with you,
    I'll be with you to the end."

Lee Fisher

Delight thyself also in the Lord; and He shall give thee the desires of thine heart.

Psalm 37 :4

SIGNS OF TRUE GREATNESS

The ability to apologize;
    to forgive and forget;
To avoid arguments;
To avoid being self-conscious;
To take snubs and reproof well;
To have mastery over the flesh;
To stoop to help others.

Anonymous

"So whatever you wish that men would do to you, do so to them."

Matthew 7:12 (RSV)

This above all: to thine own self be true,
And it must follow, as the night the day,
Thou canst not then be false to any man.

William Shakespeare

So we, being many, are one body in Christ, and every one members one of another. Having then gifts differing according to the grace that is given to us.

Romans 12:5, 6

Other people lie and cheat; we simply stretch the truth a little. Others betray; we simply protect our rights. Others steal; we borrow. Others have prejudices; we have convictions. We cry, "Those people ought to be stoned!" Jesus says, "He that is without sin among you, let him first cast a stone." Yes we are guilty of doing the same things which we accuse others of doing.

Ray C. Stedman

It is not enough to simply say, "I forgive you." You must also begin to live it out. That means acting as though their sins, like yours, have been buried in the depths of the deepest sea. If God can remember them no more, then neither should you. The reason your resentments keep coming back to you is that you keep turning them over in your mind. Please, just trust God with your thoughts. He will renew your mind.

Corrie ten Boom

The difficulties in life are intended to make us better not bitter.

Anonymous

Therefore if thou bring thy gift to the altar; and there rememberest that thy brother hath aught against thee; leave there thy gift and go thy way; first be reconciled to thy brother, and then come and offer thy gift.

Matthew 5:23, 24

Alienation from self and from one's fellow man has its roots in separation from God.

Fulton J. Sheen

BETRAYAL

Still as of old
Men by themselves are priced—
For thirty pieces Judas sold
Himself, not Christ.

Hester H. Cholmondeley

You have heard that it was said, "An eye for an eye and a tooth for a tooth." But I say to you, Do not resist one who is evil. But if any strikes you on the right cheek, turn to him the other also; and if any one would sue you and take your coat, let him have your cloak as well; and if any one forces you to go one mile, go with him two miles.

Matthew 5:38-41 (RSV)

A wise man will make haste to forgive, because he knows the true value of time, and will not suffer it to pass away in unnecessary pain.

Samuel Johnson

I am my neighbor's Bible,
He reads me when we meet,
Today he reads me in the house,
Tomorrow in the street.

He may be relative or friend,
Or slight acquaintance be,
He may not even know my name,
Yet he is reading me.

Author Unknown

Ye, shall receive power, after that the
Holy Ghost is come upon you: and ye
shall be witnesses unto me . . . unto
the uttermost part of the earth.

Acts 1 :8

We mutter, we sputter—
We fume and we spurt.
We mumble and grumble—
Our feelings get hurt.
We can't understand things—
Our vision gets dim,
When all that we need—
Is a moment with Him.

Anonymous

THE TESTING

To walk when others are running,
To whisper when others are shouting;
To sleep when others are restless,
To smile when others are angry;
To work when others are idle,
To pause when others are hurrying;
To pray when others are doubting,
To think when others are in confusion;
To face turmoil, yet feel composure;
To know inner calm in spite of everything—
This is the test of serenity.

Doris LaCasse

If we could read the secret history of our enemies, we should find in each person's life sorrow and suffering enough to disarm all hostility.

Henry Wadsworth Longfellow

There are times when I become so angry with a person that I want to say, "Get lost! You've had it!" That's the natural part of me—the limit of my human love. Then I remember how many times I've done some idiotic thing, the times I've hurt people, or the way I've misused the creation. Yet, God still loves me. He hasn't crossed me off his list, so how can I cross anybody off my list? Can't I see that when a person hurts me, he does it out of his need, his insecurity, or his pain? What good will it do for me to react to his behavior? He needs some firm ground to stand on, some resources to fill his empty bucket. Something outside of me says, "There's another way to live— keep going back in love."
It isn't easy, it isn't natural to me, and I certainly can't claim

the accomplishment for my own, but many times I am able to react in love when ordinarily I would reject in anger. The important thing is that my affirmation makes a difference not only in the life of the person who has hurt me but in my own life as well.

Louis H. Evans, Jr.

Thou God of all, whose spirit moves
From pole to silent pole,
Whose purpose binds the starry spheres
In one stupendous whole,
Whose life, like light, is freely poured
On all beneath the sun,
To thee we lift our hearts, and pray
That thou wilt make us one:

One in the patient company
Of those who heed thy will,
And steadfastly pursue the way
Of thy commandments still;
One in the holy fellowship
Of those who challenge wrong,
And lift the spirit's sword to shield
The weak against the strong;

One in the truth that makes men free,
The faith that makes men brave;
One in the love that suffers long
To seek, and serve, and save;
One in the vision of thy peace,
The kingdom yet to be,
When thou shalt be the God of all,
And all be one in thee.

John Haynes Holmes (hymn)

O God, let me not turn coward before
the difficulties of the day, or prove
recreant to its duties. Let me not
lose faith in my fellowmen. Keep me
sweet and sound of heart, in spite of
ingratitude, treachery or meanness.
Preserve me from minding little stings
or giving them.

Anonymous

O Master, let me walk with thee
In lowly paths of service free;
Tell me thy secret, help me bear
The strain of toil, the fret of care.

Help me the slow of heart to move
By some clear, winning word of love;
Teach me the wayward feet to stay,
And guide them in the homeward way.

Teach me thy patience; still with thee
In closer, dearer company,
In work that keeps faith sweet and strong,
In trust that triumphs over wrong.

Washington Gladden (hymn)

I was pretty angry by then, because I knew my actress friend
—a generous, dedicated Christian—was getting some feed-
back about the incident ... letters, telephone calls, glares,
whispered remarks. But she seemed so calm, so untroubled by
it all. She was the same warm, helpful, outgoing person I had
always known. One day I simply had to ask her about it.

"How can you take it so quietly?" I said. "Doesn't it bother
you when so many people criticize you?"

She smiled ... more concerned with my distress than her own ... and said, "Honey, I don't even see their prejudice—I just see them perfect!"

I felt tears in my eyes ... and I can feel them now as I remember how patient she was. She was no theologian, but she knew God loved her and that made all the difference in her attitude.

Colleen Townsend Evans

The middle-aged woman was afflicted with arthritis in her hands and wrists, and it was so painful that she gave up playing the piano at church. Medication helped some, but the pain persisted and even seemed to get worse. One day her doctor asked her a very personal question. "Ruth," he began, "you may choose not to answer this question, but I'm going to ask it anyway. Do you have some deep resentment or hatred in your life?"

At first the woman denied that she had any such feelings. Then her eyes filled with tears. Yes, she had a sister who she felt had cheated her in a business venture. The two women had not spoken to each other in years.

"Your physical problem could be related," the physician told her. "Even if it isn't, you are carrying some self-destructive seeds. Why not talk the matter over with your sister?"

The woman prayed about the matter for several weeks. Finally, the Lord gave her the strength to go to her sister. She forgave her and reaped all the rewards of a healed relationship. But there was more. To her surprise, her arthritis improved remarkably. Oh, it didn't go away entirely, but she began playing the piano at church again. Some say better than ever.

2.

When You Long For Beauty and Joy in Your Life

Get up early, go to the mountains and watch God make a morning. The dull gray will give way as God pushes the sun toward the horizon and there will be tints and hues of every shade as the full orbed sun bursts into view. And as the king of the day moves forward majestically flooding the earth and every lowly vale, listen to the music of heaven's choir as it sings of the majesty of God and the glory of the morning. In the hush of the earthly dawn, I hear a voice saying, "I am with you all the day. Rejoice! Rejoice!

Mrs. Charles E. Cowman

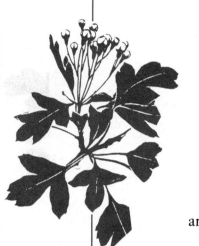

For the beauty of the earth,
For the glory of the skies,
For the love which from our birth
Over and around us lies:
    Lord of all, to Thee we raise
    This our hymn of grateful praise.

For the wonder of each hour
Of the day and of the night,
Hill and vale and tree and flower,
Sun and moon and stars of light:

For the joy of human love,
Brother, sister, parent, child;
Friends on earth and friends above;
For all gentle thoughts and mild.

Folliott S. Pierpoint   (hymn)

This is the day which the Lord hath made; we will rejoice
and be glad in it.

Psalm 118 :24

You can't do a kindness
    without a reward,
Not in silver or gold
    but in joy from the Lord—
You can't light a candle
    to show others the way
Without feeling the warmth
    of that bright little ray,
And you can't pluck a rose,
    all fragrant with dew,
Without part of its fragrance
    remaining with you.

Helen Steiner Rice

I will sing unto the Lord because He hath dealt bountifully with me.

Psalm 13 :6

I climbed the hills
through yesterday:
and I am young
and strong again;
my children climb
these hills with me,
and all the time
they shout and play;
their laughter fills
the coves among
the rhododendron and the oak
till we have struggled to
the ridge top
where the chestnuts grew.
Breathless, tired, and content
we let the mountain
breeze blow through
our busy minds
and through our hair
refresh our bodies hot and spent
and drink
from some cool mountain spring,
the view refreshing everything—
Infinity, with hills between,
silent, hazy, wild-serene.
Then...
when I return to now
I pray,
"Thank You, God,
for yesterday."

Ruth Bell Graham

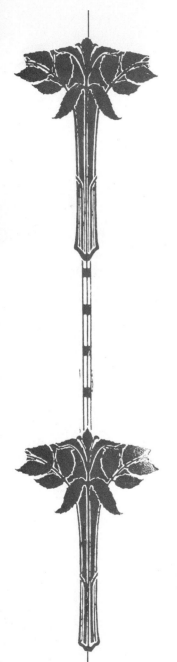

The beauty seen is partly in him who sees it.

Christian Nevell Bovee

My most cherished possession I wish I could leave you is my faith in Jesus Christ, for with Him and nothing else you can be happy, but without Him and with all else you'll never be happy.

Patrick Henry

All things bright and beautiful,
All creatures great and small,
All things wise and wonderful,
The Lord God made them all.

Cecil Frances Alexander

There was once a reed flute that served a historic church for generations, according to an old parable. Though rough to the touch and common-looking to the eye, the flute produced such beautiful music that parishioners came for miles to hear it played. Then someone decided that the instrument should be polished and decorated with gold so that its appearance would match its musical quality. Unfortunately, the gold plate affected the flute's beautiful sound, and thereafter it gave off only harsh and metallic notes. Sometimes gold has been known to destroy people in a similar way.

The world will never starve for wonders
but only for the lack of wonder.

G. K. Chesterton

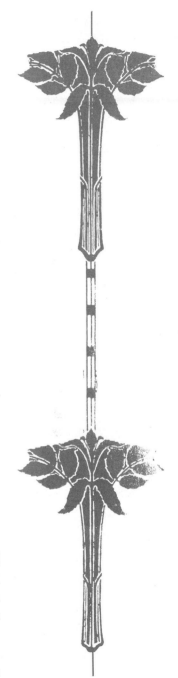

for quiet   I like unspeaking trees
for cares   a spirited mountain walk
for fulfillment   someone to please
for laughter   hearing children talk

for reassurance   a hand to hold
for strength   the persevering sea
for understanding   a friendship old
for hope   I turn to Thee

Fred Bauer

Christ be with me, Christ before me, Christ behind me,
Christ in me, Christ beneath me, Christ above me,
Christ on my right, Christ on my left,
Christ when I lie down, Christ when I sit down, Christ
    when I arise,
Christ in the heart of every man who thinks of me,
Christ in the mouth of every one who speaks of me,
Christ in every eye that sees me,
Christ in every ear that hears me.

Saint Patrick

He hath made all things beautiful.

Ecclesiastes 3 :11

As I read the Bible, I find love to be the supreme and
dominant attribute of God. The promises of God's love and
forgiveness are as real, as sure, as positive, as human words can
make them. But the total beauty of the ocean cannot be
understood until it is seen, and it is the same with God's love.
Until you actually experience it, until you actually possess it,
no one can describe its wonders to you. Never question God's

great love, for it is as unchangeable a part of God as His holiness. Were it not for the love of God, none of us would ever have a chance in the future life. But God is love! And His love for us is everlasting.

Billy Graham

Winter is past, the rain is over and gone: flowers appear on the earth: the time of the singing of birds is come.

Song of Solomon 2 :11, 12

Glory be to God for dappled things —
    For skies of couple-colour as a brinded cow;
  For rose-moles all in stipple upon trout that swim;
Fresh-firecoal chestnut-falls; finches' wings;
    Landscape plotted and pieced — fold, fallow, and plough;
    And all trades, their gear and tackle and trim.

All things counter, original, spare, strange;
    Whatever is fickle, freckled (who knows how?)
      With swift, slow; sweet, sour; adazzle, dim;
He fathers-forth whose beauty is past change;
      Praise him.

Gerard Manley Hopkins

Let us try, all of us, to come closer to that unity of spreading Christ's love wherever we go. Love and compassion; have deep compassion for the people. People are suffering much: mentally, physically, in every possible way. So you are the ones to bring that hope, that love, that kindness. Do you want to do something beautiful for God? There is a person who needs you. This is your chance.

Mother Teresa

In all ranks of life the human heart yearns
for the beautiful; and the beautiful things
that God makes are His gift to all alike.

Harriet Beecher Stowe

Now you are happy with the inexpressible joy that comes
from heaven itself.

I Peter 1 :8 (Living Bible)

One midnight deep in starlight still
   I dreamed that I received this bill:
". . . In account with life:
Five thousand breathless dawns all new;
Five thousand flowers fresh in dew;
Five thousand sunsets wrapped in gold;
One million snowflakes served ice cold;
Five quiet friends; one baby's love;
One white mad sea with clouds above;
One hundred music-haunted dreams
   Of moon-drenched roads and hurrying streams,
   Of prophesying winds and trees,
   Of silent stars and drowsing bees;
One June night in a fragrant wood;
One heart that loved and understood."
   I wondered when I waked at day
   How—in God's name—I could pay.

Courtland W. Sayres

The little boy was fishing with his grandfather on the banks
of a river. Their conversation covered everything from where
fish go at night to why the sun is so red on the horizon. In the

stillness and beauty that come in summer twilight, the boy asked, "Gramps, can anyone see God?"

"Laurie," his grandfather answered, "it's getting so I can't see anything *but* God."

This is my Father's world;
And to my listening ears
All nature sings, and 'round me rings
The music of the spheres.
This is my Father's world;
I rest me in the thought
Of rocks and trees, of skies and seas,
His hand the wonders wrought.

This is my Father's world;
The birds their carols raise,
The morning light, the lily white,
Declare their Maker's praise.
This is my Father's world;
He shines in all that's fair;
In the rustling grass I hear Him pass;
He speaks to me everywhere.

Maltbie D. Babcock   (hymn)

A BEAUTIFUL CRYSTAL CATHEDRAL

"What's the most fun for a surfer?" I queried a young man one day on a beach in Hawaii.

"Shooting the tube," he replied.

"How's that done?" I asked.

"Well, you ride the top of the wave," he began, making the arc of the wave with his free hand, "until it begins to lap over you and you go right down the tube of the wave. It's like being in a beautiful crystal cathedral. The sun sparkles down through the water and it's all around you. The noise of the thundering surf is deafening, and the speed is breathtaking."

"What if you lose your balance and fall?" I asked.

It's like being in a huge washing machine — tumbling helplessly to possible death or injury." he answered.

As he talked, I realized that he had the same kind of enthusiasm for "shooting the tube" that some people have for their Christian ministry. No amount of time, money or personal danger is too much. Those who play it safe by sitting on the beach may get a casual thrill, but they miss the thundering excitement of entering the arena and getting involved.

The New Testament approach is to get in the action with everything you have and are. To "shoot the tube" for the Lord.

Bill Glass

> Rejoice in glorious hope;
> Jesus, the Judge, shall come
> And take his servants up
> To their eternal home.
>
> Lift up your heart.
> Lift up your voice;
> Rejoice, he bids
> His saints rejoice!

Abraham Lincoln

If you keep my commandments, you will abide in my love... These things I have spoken to you, that my joy may be in you, and that your joy may be full.

John 15:10, 11 (RSV)

God's gifts put man's best dreams to shame.

Elizabeth Barrett Browning

To God be the glory—great things He hath done!
So loved He the world that He gave us His Son,
Who yielded His life an atonement for sin,
And opened the lifegate that all may go in.

Praise the Lord, praise the Lord,
Let the earth hear His voice!
Praise the Lord, praise the Lord,
Let the people rejoice!
O come to the Father thru Jesus the Son,
And give Him the glory—great things He hath done!

Fanny J. Crosby (hymn)

Jesus Christ is risen today, Alleluia!
Our triumphant holy day, Alleluia!
Who did once upon the cross, Alleluia!
Suffer to redeem our loss. Alleluia!

Latin hymn of 14th century

There is sunshine in my soul today,
More glorious and bright
Than glows in any earthly sky,
For Jesus is my light.

There is gladness in my soul today,
And hope and praise and love,
For blessings which He gives me now,
For joys laid up above.

Eliza E. Hewitt (hymn)

Beauty seen is never lost,
God's colors all are fast;

The glory of this sunset heaven
Into my soul has passed.

Alfred, Lord Tennyson

The pleasantest things in the world are pleasant thoughts;
and the great art of life is to have as many of them as possible.

Michel de Montaigne

The love of God is greater far
Than tongue or pen can ever tell;
It goes beyond the highest star,
And reaches to the lowest hell.
The guilty pair, bowed down with care,
God gave His Son to win;
His erring child He reconciled,
And pardoned from his sin.

O love of God, how rich and pure!
How measureless and strong!
It shall for evermore endure
The saints' and angels' song.

Could we with ink the ocean fill,
And were the skies of parchment made,
Were every stalk on earth a quill,
And every man a scribe by trade,
To write the love of God above
Would drain the ocean dry
Nor could the scroll contain the whole,
Though stretched from sky to sky.

F. M. Lehman (hymn)

Lord of all being, throned afar,
Thy glory flames from sun and star;
Center and soul of every sphere,
Yet to each loving heart how near!

Sun of our life, thy quickening ray
Sheds on our path the glow of day;
Star of our hope, thy softened light
Cheers the long watches of the night.

Oliver Wendell Holmes (hymn)

'I pray thee, O God, that I may be beautiful within.'

Socrates

O worship the King, all glorious above,
O gratefully sing his power and his love;
Our Shield and Defender, the Ancient of Days,
Pavilioned in splendor, and girded with praise.

O tell of his might, O sing of his grace,
Whose robe is the light, whose canopy space;
His chariots of wrath the deep thunderclouds form,
And dark is his path on the wings of the storm.

The earth with its stores of wonders untold,
Almighty, thy power hath founded of old,
Hath stablished it fast by a changeless decree,
And round it hath cast like a mantle, the sea.

Frail children of dust, and feeble as frail,
In thee do we trust, nor find thee to fail;
Thy mercies how tender how firm to the end,
Our Maker, Defender, Redeemer, and Friend!

Robert Grant (hymn)

Guide me, O thou great Jehovah,
Pilgrim through this barren land;
I am weak, but thou art mighty;
Hold me with thy powerful hand.

William Williams (hymn)

The year's at the spring
The day's at the morn;
Morning's at seven;
The hillside's dew-pearled;
The lark's on the wing;
The snail's on the thorn;
God's in his heaven—
All's right with the world.

Robert Browning

Serene will be our days and bright,
And happy will our nature be,
When love is an unerring light,
And joy its own security.
And they a blissful course may hold
Even now, who, not unwisely bold,
Live in the spirit of this creed;
Yet seek thy firm support, according to their need.

William Wordsworth

ETERNAL LIFE

It was unspeakable love that thought it.
It was unspeakable life that bought it.
It was unspeakable death that wrought it.
There is unspeakable joy where He brought it.

Anonymous

43

Hitherto have ye asked nothing in my name: ask,
and ye shall receive, that your joy may be full.

John 16 :24

The best marriages I know are those in which the husband
and wife build on the best in each other... the honest facing of
weaknesses without the need to linger over them ... no at-
tempts to change each other... but rather a loving acceptance
of each as a whole person ... support for the direction each
one's life is taking... an ability to share and take delight in the
warm feeling that comes with the good things that happen to
each. These couples are so filled with the love of God in their
individual lives that they simply must give of that love to each
other... And while these things need not be spoken in so many
words, the joy they bring each other is constantly communi-
cated.

Colleen Townsend Evans

When the Lord turned again the captivity
    of Zion, we were like them that dream.
Then was our mouth filled with laughter,
    and our tongue with singing... The Lord hath
done great things for us; whereof we are glad.

Psalm 126 : 1-3 KJV

I thank Thee, my Creator and Lord, that Thou hast given
me these joys in Thy creation, this ecstasy over the works of
Thy hands. I have made known the glory of Thy works to men
as far as my finite spirit was able to comprehend Thy infinity. If
I have said anything wholly unworthy of Thee, or have aspired
after my own glory, graciously forgive me.

Johann Kepler

3.

When You Are Fearful and Worried About What Tomorrow Will Bring

Several years ago, shortly after an earthquake had struck southern California, Cliff Barrows talked with Ethel Waters, who had experienced it in her fifteenth-floor Los Angeles apartment. "How did you get along during the big scare, Ethel?" Cliff inquired.

"When I woke up, the ceiling was going every which way," she answered. "I said, 'Whatever you have in mind for me is all right, Lord. You've got my address and I've got Yours'."

God of our life, through all the circling
years, we trust in Thee;
In all the past, through all our hopes
and fears, Thy hand we see.
With each new day, when morning lifts
the veil,
We own Thy mercies, Lord, which never
fail.

Hugh T. Kerr   (hymn)

He that dwelleth in the secret place of the most High shall
abide under the shadow of the Almighty.
I will say of the Lord, He is my refuge and my fortress: my
God; in him will I trust.
Surely he shall deliver thee from the snare of the fowler, and
from the noisome pestilence.
He shall cover thee with his feathers, and under his wings
shalt thou trust: his truth shall be thy shield and buckler.
Thou shalt not be afraid for the terror by night; nor for the
arrow that flieth by day;
Nor for the pestilence that walketh in darkness; nor for the
destruction that wasteth at noonday.
A thousand shall fall at thy side, and ten thousand at thy right
hand; but it shall not come nigh thee.
Only with thine eyes shalt thou behold and see the reward of
the wicked.
Because thou hast made the Lord, which is my refuge, even
the most High, thy habitation;
There shall no evil befall thee, neither shall any plague come
nigh thy dwelling.
For he shall give his angels charge over thee, to keep thee in
all thy ways.

They shall bear thee up in their hands, lest thou dash thy foot
  against a stone.
Thou shalt tread upon the lion and adder: the young lion and
  the dragon shalt thou trample under feet.
Because he hath set his love upon me, therefore will I deliver
  him: I will set him on high, because he hath known my
  name.
He shall call upon me, and I will answer him: I will be with
  him in trouble; I will deliver him, and honour him.
With long life will I satisfy him, and shew him my salvation.

Psalm 91

Fear knocked on the door.
Faith answered.
No one was there.

Anonymous

Keep Thou my feet; I do not ask to see
The distant scene—one step enough for me.

John Newman   (hymn)

In 1735, a young John Wesley was on his way from England
to America to preach the gospel to Indians. His ship encountered heavy seas, and the evangelist was very fearful. A fellow
passenger seemed oblivious of the storm, so Wesley asked
him, "Aren't you afraid?"
  "No, I know Jesus Christ. Do you?"
  Wesley realized for the first time that he did not really know
Christ as his personal Saviour, and he turned his life over to
Him.

At night, my weary body aches,
My mind is torn by questions deep,
But while I rest my Father takes
And mends my raveled soul with sleep.

Fred Bauer

Fear not, for I am with thee.

Isaiah 41 :10

Amazing grace! How sweet the sound—
That saved a wretch like me!
I once was lost but now am found,
Was blind but now I see.

'Twas grace that taught my heart to fear,
And grace my fears relieved;
How precious did that grace appear
The hour I first believed!

The Lord has promised good to me,
His word my hope secures;
He will my shield and portion be
As long as life endures.

Through many dangers, toils, and snares,
I have already come;
'Tis grace hath brought me safe thus far,
And grace will lead me home.

John Newton   (hymn)

Go to sleep, God is awake.

Victor Hugo

I have lived, Sir, a long time, and the longer I live, the more convincing proofs I see of this truth—that God governs in the affairs of men. And if a sparrow cannot fall to the ground without His notice, is it probable that an empire can rise without His aid?

Benjamin Franklin

Just close your eyes and open your heart
And feel your worries and cares depart,
Just yield yourself to the Father above
And let Him hold you secure in HIS love—

Helen Steiner Rice

Courage is fear that has said its prayers.

Anonymous

He giveth power to the faint: and to them that have no might he increaseth strength.

Isaiah 40 :29

And I said to the man who stood at the
    gate of the year;
Give me a light that I may tread safely
    into the unknown!
And he replied: Go out into the darkness!
    and put thine hand into the hand of God.
That shall be for thee better than light,
    and safer than a known way.

M. Louise Haskins

Life is a concrete fact, filled with abundance. Fill your mind with the blessings of life and there will be no room for fear.

John Glossinger

OUR BURDEN BEARER

The little sharp vexations
   And the briars that cut the feet,
Why not take all to the Helper
   Who has never failed us yet?
Tell Him about the heartache,
   And tell Him the longings too,
Tell Him the baffled purpose
   When we scarce know what to do.
Then, leaving all our weakness
   With the One divinely strong,
Forget that we bore the burden
   And carry away the song.

Phillips Brooks

Let not your heart be troubled, neither let it be afraid.

John 14 :27

You cannot merely resolve, "I will not worry." There is no casting your anxiety and leaving your mind a blank ... The practical cure is recommended by Jesus: replace worry by trust. "Let not your heart be troubled," said Jesus. The word means literally to be torn apart, to be divided. Put all your heart in one place; believe in God. The cure for worry is a deeper knowledge of God.

Kenneth J. Foreman

Courage is resistance to fear, mastery of fear—not absence of fear.

Mark Twain

> Safe in the arms of Jesus,
> Safe in His gentle breast,
> There by His love o'ershadowed,
> Sweetly my soul shall rest.

Fanny J. Crosby (hymn)

God shall supply all your needs according to his riches in glory.

Philippians 4 :19

Lay not up for yourselves treasures on earth, where moth and rust doth corrupt, and where thieves break through and steal:

But lay up for yourselves treasures in heaven, where neither moth nor rust doth corrupt, and where thieves do not break through nor steal.

For where your treasure is, there will your heart be also. . . .

Take no thought for your life, what ye shall eat, or what ye shall drink; nor yet for your body, what ye shall put on. Is not the life more than meat, and the body than raiment?

Behold the fowls of the air: for they sow not, neither do they reap, nor gather into barns; yet your heavenly Father feedeth them. Are ye not much better than they?

Which of you by taking thought can add one cubit unto his stature?

And why take ye thought for raiment? Consider the lilies of the field, how they grow; they toil not, neither do they spin:

And yet I say unto you, That even Solomon in all his glory

was not arrayed like one of these.

Wherefore, if God so clothe the grass of the field, which to day is, and to morrow is cast unto the oven, shall he not much more clothe you, O ye of little faith?

Therefore, take no thought, saying, What shall we eat? or What shall we drink? or, Wherewithal shall we be clothed?

(For after all these things do the Gentiles seek:) for your heavenly Father knoweth that ye have need of all these things.

But seek ye first the kingdom of God, and his righteousness; and all these things shall be added unto you.

Take therefore no thought for the morrow: for the morrow shall take thought of the things of itself. Sufficient unto the day is the evil thereof.

Matthew 6 : 19-21, 25-34

Lord,
help me not to dread
what might happen,
not to worry about
what could happen,
but to accept what does happen.
Because You care for me.

Dorothy Morritt

God sent His Son, they called Him Jesus;
He came to love, heal, and forgive;
He lived and died to buy my pardon,
An empty grave is there to prove my Savior lives.

   Because He lives I can face tomorrow;
   Because He lives all fear is gone;
   Because I know He holds the future.
   And life is worth the living just because He lives!

How sweet to hold a newborn baby,
And feel the pride and joy He gives;
But greater still the calm assurance,
This child can face uncertain days because He lives.

And then one day I'll cross the river;
I'll fight life's final war with pain;
And then as death gives way to victory,
I'll see the lights of glory and I'll know He lives.

Gloria and William J. Gaither   (hymn)

O Lord, what Thou sayest is true. Greater is Thy anxiety for me than all the care that I can take for myself. For he stands very unsteadily who casts not all his anxiety upon Thee.

Thomas à Kempis

When my heart is overwhelmed: lead me to the rock that is higher than I.

Psalm 61 :2

TIME IS

Too Slow for those who Wait,
Too Swift for those who Fear,
Too Long for those who Grieve,
Too Short for those who Rejoice;
    But for those who Love,
    Time is eternity.

Henry Van Dyke

Not one sparrow can fall to the ground without your Father knowing it.

Matthew 10:29 (Living Bible)

Some time ago, a businessman drew up what he called a "Worry Chart," in which he kept a record of his worries. He discovered that 40 percent of them were about things that probably would never happen; 30 percent concerned past decisions that he could not now unmake; 12 percent dealt with other people's criticisms of him; 10 percent were worries about his health. He concluded that only 8 percent of them were really legitimate.

Francis C. Ellis

For God hath not given us the spirit of fear; but of power, and of love, and of a sound mind.

II Timothy 1:7

Build a little fence of trust
   Around today;
Fill each space with loving work
   And therein stay;
Look not through the sheltering bars
   Upon tomorrow,
God will help thee bear what comes,
   Of joy or sorrow.

Mary Frances Butts

The function of fear is to warn us of danger; not to make us afraid to face it.

Anonymous

OVERHEARD IN AN ORCHARD

Said the Robin to the Sparrow:
　"I should really like to know
Why these anxious human beings
　Rush about and worry so."

Said the sparrow to the Robin:
　"Friend, I think that it must be
That they have no heavenly Father
　Such as cares for you and me."

Elizabeth Cheney

Cast thy burden upon the Lord, and He shall sustain thee: he shall never suffer the righteous to be moved.

Psalm 55 :22

Be not afraid of sudden fear, neither of the desolation of the wicked, when it cometh. For the Lord shall be thy confidence, and shall keep thy foot from being taken.

Proverbs 3 :25-26

Coward and wayward and weak,
I change with the changing sky.
Today so eager and brave,
Tomorrow not willing to try.
But He never gives in,
And we two will win,
Jesus and I.

Unknown Author

Jesus, Savior, pilot me
Over life's tempestuous sea;
Unknown waves before me roll,
Hiding rock and treacherous shoal;
Chart and compass come from thee;
Jesus, Savior, pilot me.

As a mother stills her child,
Thou canst hush the ocean wild;
Boisterous waves obey thy will
When thou sayest to them, "Be still."
Wondrous Sovereign of the sea,
Jesus, Savior, pilot me.

When at last I near the shore,
And the fearful breakers roar
'Twixt me and the peaceful rest,
Then, while leaning on thy breast,
May I hear thee say to me,
"Fear not, I will pilot thee."

Edward Hopper (hymn)

I was at the end of my first week in America and practically at the end of my money. The clerk at the YWCA told me I could not stay there another week. Where should she forward my mail?

"I don't know yet. God has a room for me but He has not told me where yet."

I could see by the look on her face that she was concerned about me. Then she handed me a piece of mail which she had overlooked. The letter was from a woman who heard me speak in New York. She was offering me the use of her son's room.

I gave the amazed clerk my new address after thanking God for His care.

Corrie ten Boom

The Lord is my shepherd; I shall not want.
He maketh me to lie down in green pastures;
 he leadeth me beside the still waters.
He restoreth my soul: he leadeth me in
 the paths of righteousness for his name's sake.
Yea, though I walk through the valley of
 the shadow of death, I will fear no
 evil: for thou art with me; thy rod and
 thy staff they comfort me.
Thou preparest a table before me in the
 presence of mine enemies: thou anointest
 my head with oil; my cup runneth over.
Surely goodness and mercy shall follow
 me all the days of my life: and I will
 dwell in the house of the Lord for ever.

Psalm 23

We cannot go where God is not,
and where God is, all is well.

Anonymous

At the cathedral in Milan, Italy, three significant inscriptions surmount the doorway. Over the right-hand portal is a sculptured wreath of flowers with the proverb, "All that pleases is but for a moment." Over the left-hand entrance are a cross and a crown under which are the words, "All that troubles is but for a moment." Then over the central door is a simple sentence: "Nothing is important save that which is eternal."

Stephen F. Olford

GOD'S SUNSHINE

Never once—since the world began —
Has the sun ever stopped shining;
And we grumbled at his inconstancy,
But the clouds were really to blame, not he,
  For behind them he was shining.

And so—behind life's darkest clouds
  God's love is always shining;
We veil it at times with our faithless fears,
And darken our sight with our foolish tears,
But in time the atmosphere always clears,
For His love is always shining.

John Oxenham

Once when Stonewall Jackson planned a daring attack, one of his generals fearfully objected, saying:"I am afraid of this"or "I fear that . . . ." Putting his hand on his timorous subordinate's shoulder, Jackson said, "General, never take counsel of your fears."

Norman Vincent Peale

Let nothing disturb thee,
Nothing affright thee;
All things are passing;
God never changeth;
Patient endurance
Attaineth to all things.
Who God possesseth
In nothing is wanting:
Alone God sufficeth.

Saint Theresa

4.

When You Have Lost A Loved One

Writing on the subject of fearing death, Leslie Weatherhead, noted English writer and preacher, once drew a parallel between the beginning of life and what is often perceived to be the end. A baby would never choose on its own to leave the security of its mother's womb, so safe, so secure, so warm, he said. But Nature prevails and when the time is right the baby is sent forth into the uncertain an unknown. But what a surprise awaits the child—a loving mother holds it close to her warm body and she feeds it and cares for its

every need. All around are people who shower affection upon it.

Is it not much the same at death, Weatherhead speculated. Again, we are reluctant to leave, reluctant to embark on an unchartered journey into an unknown land. But if the Bible is true, there awaits for all who believe in Jesus a wonderful welcome, full of affectionate reunions, full of joy and unprecedented love and peace. With such a prospect in store, we need have no fear of death.

For all the saints who from their labors rest,
Who Thee by faith before the world confessed,
Thy name, O Jesus, be forever blest:
Alleluia! Alleluia!

Thou wast their rock, their fortress, and their might,
Thou, Lord, their captain in the well-fought fight;
Thou, in the darkness drear, their one true light:
Alleluia! Alleluia!

O may Thy soldiers, faithful, true and bold,
Fight as the saints who nobly fought of old,
And win with them the victor's crown of gold:
Alleluia! Alleluia!

O blest communion, fellowship divine:
We feebly struggle, they in glory shine;
Yet all are one in Thee, for all are Thine:
Alleluia! Alleluia

But Lo! there breaks a yet more glorious day;
The saints triumphant rise in bright array;

The King of glory passes on His way:
Alleluia! Alleluia!

From earth's wide bounds, from ocean's farthest coast,
Through gates of pearl streams in the countless host,
Singing to Father, Son, and Holy Ghost:
Alleluia! Alleluia!

William W. How (hymn)

If God hath made this world so fair
Where sin and death abound,
How beautiful beyond compare
Will paradise be found.

James Montgomery

So live, that when thy summons comes to join
The innumerable caravan, which moves
To that mysterious realm, where each shall take
His chamber in the silent halls of death,
Thou go not, like the quarry-slave at night,
Scourged to his dungeon, but, sustained and soothed
By an unfalterng trust, approach thy grave
Like one who wraps the drapery of his couch
About him, and lies down to pleasant dreams.

William Cullen Bryant

When I must leave you
   for a little while,
Please do not grieve
   and shed wild tears
And hug your sorrow
   to you through the years,

But start out bravely
    with a gallant smile;
And for my sake
    and in my name
Live on and do
    all the things the same,
Feed not your loneliness
    on empty days,
But fill each waking hour
    in useful ways,
Reach out your hand
    in comfort and in cheer
And I in turn will comfort you
    and hold you near;
And never, never
    be afraid to die,
For I am waiting
    for you in the sky!

Helen Steiner Rice

Blessed are they that mourn: for they shall be comforted.

Matthew 5:4

CONSOLATION

He is not dead, this friend; not dead,
But, in the path we mortals tread,
Gone some few, trifling steps ahead,
And nearer to the end:
So that you, too, once past the bend,
Shall meet again, as face to face, this friend
You fancy dead.

Robert Louis Stevenson

For God so loved the world, that he gave his only begotten Son, that whosoever believeth in him should not perish, but have everlasting life.

John 3:16

Let us learn like a bird for a moment to take
Sweet rest on a branch that is ready to break;
She feels the branch tremble, yet gaily she sings.
What is it to her? She has wings, she has wings!

Victor Hugo

He leadeth me, O blessed thought!
O words with heav'nly comfort fraught!
Whate'er I do, where'er I be,
Still 'tis God's hand that leadeth me.

He leadeth me, He leadeth me,
By his own hand He leadeth me;
His faithful follower I would be,
For by His hand He leadeth me.

And when my task on earth is done,
When by Thy grace the victory's won,
E'en death's cold wave I will not flee,
Since God thru Jordan leadeth me.

Joseph H. Gilmore (hymn)

THE SHIP

I am standing on the seashore. A ship at my side spreads her white sails to the morning breezes and departs for the blue ocean. She is an object of beauty and strength, and I stand and watch her until at last she is only a ribbon of white cloud just

where the sea and sky come to mingle with each other.

Then someone at my side says, "There, she's gone!" Gone where? Gone from my sight—that is all. She is just as large in mast and hull and spar as she was when she left my side, and just as able to bear her load of living freight to the place of destination.

Her diminished size is in me, not in her; and just at the moment when someone at my side says, "There, she's gone!" there are other eyes watching her coming, and other voices ready to take up the glad shout, "There she comes!"

And that is what people call dying.

Author Unknown

Life is real! Life is earnest!
And the grave is not its goal;
Dust thou art, to dust returnest
Was not spoken of the soul.

Henry Wadsworth Longfellow

As parents, we are called upon sometimes to explain some of life's mysteries to our children. When our daughter, Tina, was six, she was saddened about the death of one of our friends and asked, "Does a body in a coffin mind being buried?" I was carefully composing an answer when I remembered an experience our family had shared a short time before.

We'd found a cicada clinging to a tree. Unlike most times when only the transparent shell remained, in this instance the insect was still inside. We put it in a jar, spent time watching it and were thrilled the next morning to see that a magnificent creature with wings had emerged. Taking the jar outside, we opened it and watched the cicada fly free, high overhead, shimmering in the bright sunlight. The only evidence we had of our brief pet was the empty shell it had left behind.

I reminded Tina of our visitor and asked if she thought the shell would mind being buried.

"No," Tina quickly replied, "because the insect isn't in it."

"That's the same way it is with the body of someone who loved Jesus. Only their shell remains." Tina's soft smile showed that she'd understood.

Linda Gramatky Smith

Yea, though I walk through the valley
of the shadow of death,
I will fear no evil: for thou art with me.

Psalm 23 :4

I feel as if I am intruding among posterity when I ought to be abed and asleep. I look upon death to be as necessary to the constitution as sleep. We shall arise refreshed in the morning.

Benjamin Franklin

If death were not a beginning
Then life would be an end
And the cattails and the tall grass
And the dew that hangs on lovers' eyes
Would all be monstrous and the grave
Would be a stillborn child.
But the night
As out of the mouth the poem
Comes a quite wild and howling child
Whose name was Christ
And blessed with the stars
He tells his thrice and million
And more than million glory
To any mother, lover, or listener.
Listen to resurrection sing.
But out of the night
The White Lamb in the Word is Still.

John Tagliabue

There's a wideness in God's mercy
Like the wideness of the sea;
There's a kindness in His justice
Which is more than liberty.

For the love of God is broader
Than the measure of man's mind,
And the heart of the Eternal
Is most wonderfully kind.

Frederick W. Faber   (hymn)

Christ the Lord is risen today,
Sons of men and angels say:
Raise your joys and triumphs high,
Sing, ye heavens, and earth reply:
Alleluia!

Lives again our glorious King,
Where, O death, is now thy sting?
Dying once, He all doth save,
Where thy victory, O grave?
Allelulia!

Love's redeeming work is done,
Fought the fight, the battle won,
Death in vain forbids Him rise,
Christ has opened paradise,
Alleluia!

Charles Wesley (hymn)

Death is only an old door
   Set in a garden wall.
On quiet hinges it gives at dusk,
   When the thrushes call.

Along the lintel are green leaves,

Beyond, the light lies still;
Very weary and willing feet
   Go over that sill.

There is nothing to trouble any heart,
   Nothing to hurt at all.
Death is only an old door
   In a garden wall.

                Nancy Byrd Turner

She was a beautiful three-year-old child, and her parents were distraught when they lost her in a freak accident. Unable to justify this tragedy with their concept of a loving God, they went to their minister for help. "Why?" they asked. His answers did not relieve their grief. So they sought out a church deacon. He quoted many verses of Scripture, trying to give them comfort, but his words fell on deaf ears.

They finally turned to a saintly old woman in the church. She had little formal education, but she knew her Bible well. Surely *she* could give them a spiritual answer. After hearing the details of the child's death, the old woman didn't utter a single word. She simply and tenderly wrapped her arms around the heartbroken couple's shoulders, and together they cried the hurt away.

Don't talk to me yet;
the wound is fresh,
the nauseous pain
I can't forget
fades into numbness
like a wave,
then comes again.
Your tears I understand,

but grief is deaf;
it cannot hear the words
you gently planned
and tried to say.
But...
pray.

Ruth Bell Graham

Let not you heart be troubled: ye believe in
  God, believe also in me.
In my Father's house are many mansions: if it were
  not so, I would have told you. I go to prepare
  a place for you.
And if I go and prepare a place for you, I will come
  again, and receive you unto myself; that where I
  am, there ye may be also.

John 14:1-3

UPHILL

Does the road wind uphill all the way?
Yes, to the very end.
Will the day's journey take the whole day long?
From morn to night, my friend.

But is there for the night a resting-place?
A roof for when the slow, dark hours begin.
May not the darkness hide it from my face?
You cannot miss that inn.

Shall I meet other wayfarers at night?
Those who have gone before.
Then must I knock, or call when just in sight?
They will not keep you waiting at the door.

Shall I find comfort, travel-sore and weak?
Of labour you shall find the sum.
Will there be beds for me and all who seek?
Yea, beds for all who come.

Christina Rossetti

God sometimes passes us into the valley of shadow that we may learn the way, and know how to lead others through it into the light. To get comfort, we must comfort with the comfort wherewith we ourselves have been comforted. In wiping the tears of others our own will cease to fall.

F. B. Meyer

Day is done, gone the sun
From the lake, from the hill, from the sky.
All is well, safely rest,
God is nigh.

Anonymous

One of the great bonuses of being a Christian is the great hope that extends beyond the grave into the glory of God's tomorrow. A little girl was running toward the cemetery as the darkness of evening began to fall. She passed a friend who asked her if she was not afraid to go through the graveyard at night. "Oh, no," she said, "I'm not afraid. My home is just on the other side!" We Christians are not afraid of the night of death because our heavenly home is "just on the other side." The resurrection of Christ changed the midnight of bereavement into a sunrise of reunion.

Billy Graham

Death, be not proud, though some have called thee
Mighty and dreadful, for thou art not so:
For those whom thou think'st thou dost overthrow
Die not, poor Death; nor yet canst thou kill me.
From rest and sleep, which but thy picture be,
Much pleasure; then from thee much more must flow;
And soonest our best men with thee do go—
Rest of their bones and souls' delivery!
Thou'rt slave to fate, chance, kings, and desperate men,
And dost with poison, war, and sickness dwell;
And poppy or charms can make us sleep as well
And better than thy stroke. Why swell'st thou then?
  One short sleep past, we wake eternally,
  And Death shall be no more: Death, thou shalt die!

John Donne

The death of a 12-year-old son sent his mother into such a siege of grief that she withdrew from all outside activity, even though she had always been extremely busy in church and community affairs.

It didn't seem as if she would ever shake the sorrow until one night she had a dream that changed everything. In her dream the woman saw a procession of children, dressed in white, carrying unlit candles. One by one, the children moved up to Christ, who would light their candles. But when it was her son's turn, the child drew back.

"Son," the woman called out in her dream, "why don't you allow Christ to light your candle?"

The boy turned to her and said, "Mother, I am not permitted to light my candle as long as you are so sad." The next day his mother put aside her grief, returned to the work of her church and served the Lord with an enthusiasm and radiance that never left the rest of her life.

IN MEMORY OF A CHILD

The angels guide him now,
And watch his curly head,
And lead him in their games,
The little boy we led.

He cannot come to harm,.
He knows more than we know,
His light is brighter far
Than daytime here below.

His path leads on and on,
Through pleasant lawns and flowers,
His brown eyes open wide
At grass more green than ours.

With playmates like himself,
The shining boy will sing,
Exploring wondrous woods,
Sweet with eternal spring.

Vachel Lindsay

Father, I am only human. I need the touch of human companionship. Sorely I miss those I love who are with Thee.

I pray, O Jesus, that Thou wilt reveal to me unseen presences. Help me to know how close my loved ones are. For if they are with Thee, and Thou art with me, I know that they cannot be far away.

Make real for me that contact of spirit with spirit that will re-establish the lost fellowship for which my heart yearns. Give to me faith shining through my heart. Point me with joy to the great reunion.

But until then, enable me to live happily and worthily of those who are with Thee. In the Name of Him who is the Lord of Life, I pray, Amen.

Peter Marshall

73

Tony, eight years old, was in Mrs. Smith's Sunday School class. Tony was considered retarded. He was slow in reading, his numbers did not come out right and his clumsiness made the other boys laugh. On Palm Sunday, Mrs. Smith told the story of Jesus' resurrection, emphasizing that the tomb was empty when the two Marys arrived Easter morning. At the end of the lesson, she gave each boy a plastic egg and asked them to bring back their eggs the next Sunday with something inside that represented life. The following Sunday, Easter, the children were eager to "show and tell" about the contents of their eggs. One boy had soil in his, explaining that soil makes things grow. Another child had rocks. A third had flowers. It was Tony's turn, but when he opened his egg, it was empty. One boy exclaimed, "Tony doesn't understand what we were to do." Another said, "He's too dumb." Mrs. Smith said, "Let's give Tony a chance to explain." Gently she took his hand, "Tony, you tell us about your egg." Tony replied, "Last Sunday you told us that the tomb was empty and that Jesus is alive. The angel said, 'He is not here. He is risen.' My empty egg is like the empty tomb."

Bertha Erickson

God of the living, in whose eyes
Unveiled thy whole creation lies,
All souls are thine; we must not say
That those are dead who pass away;
From this our world of flesh set free,
We know them living unto thee.

Released from earthly toil and strife,
With thee is hidden still their life;
Thine are their thoughts, their works, their powers,
All thine, and yet most truly ours,
For well we know, where'er they be,
Our dead are living unto thee.

Thy word is true, thy will is just;
To thee we leave them, Lord, in trust,
And bless thee for the love which gave
Thy Son to fill a human grave,
That none might fear that world to see,
Where all are living unto thee.

John Ellerton (hymn)

I do not fear death. Often I wake in the night and think of it. I look forward to it with a thrill of joyful expectation and anticipation, which would become impatience were it not that Jesus is my Master as well as my Savior. I feel I have work to do for Him that I would not shirk, and also that His time to call me home will be the best and right time, and therefore I am content to wait.

I could not do without Jesus. I cannot and I do not live without Him. It is a new and different life, and this life which takes away all fear of death is what I want others to have and enjoy.

Frances Ridley Havergal

GETHSEMANE

All those who journey, soon or late,
Must pass within the garden's gate;
Must kneel alone in darkness there,
And battle with some fierce despair.
God pity those who cannot say:
"Not mine but thine"; who only pray:
"Let this cup pass," and cannot see
The purpose in Gethsemane.

Ella Wheeler Wilcox

Father, to thee we look in all our sorrow;
Thou art the fountain whence our healing flows;
Dark though the night, joy cometh with the morrow;
Safety they rest who on thy love repose.

When fond hopes fail and skies are dark before us,
When the vain cares that vex our life increase,
Comes with its calm the thought that thou art o'er us,
And we grow quiet, folded in thy peace.

Nought shall affright us, on thy goodness leaning;
Low in the heart faith singeth still her song;
Chastened by pain we learn life's deeper meaning,
And in our weakness thou dost make us strong.

Patient, O heart, though heavy be thy sorrows,
Be not cast down, disquieted in vain;
Yet shall thou praise him, when these darkened furrows,
Where now he ploweth, wave with golden grain.

Frederick L. Hosmer (hymn)

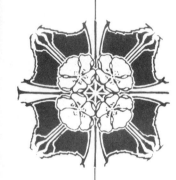

SOMEBODY'S DARLING

Into a ward of the whitewashed halls,
   Where the dead and dying lay,
Wounded by bayonets, shells and balls,
   Somebody's Darling was borne one day.
Somebody's Darling, so young and so brave,
   Wearing yet on his pale, sweet face,
Soon to be hid by the dust of the grave,
   The lingering light of his boyhood's grace.

Matted and damp are the curls of gold,
   Kissing the snow of the fair young brow;
Pale are the lips of delicate mould—
   Somebody's Darling is dying now.
Back from his beautiful blue-veined brow,

Brush all the wandering waves of gold;
Cross his hand on his bosom now—
    Somebody's Darling is still and cold.

Kiss him once for somebody's sake,
    Murmur a prayer both soft and low;
One bright curl from his fair mates take—
    They were somebody's pride, you know;
Somebody's hand hath rested there—
    Was it a mother's soft and white?
And have the lips of a sister fair
    Been baptized in the waves of light?

God knows best! He has somebody's love;
    Somebody's heart enshrined him there;
Somebody wafted his name above,
    Night and morn, on the wings of prayer.
Somebody wept when he marched away,
    Looking so handsome, brave and grand,
Somebody's kiss on his forehead lay,
    Somebody clung to his parting hand.

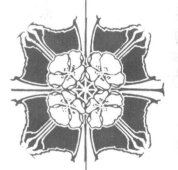

Somebody's waiting and watching for him—
    Yearning to hold him again to her heart;
And there he lies with his blue eyes dim,
    And the smiling child-like lips apart.
Tenderly bury the fair young dead,
    Pausing to drop on his grave a tear.
Carve in the wooden slab at his head:
    "Somebody's Darling lies sleeping here."

Marie R. LaCoste

For the believer who has been to the Cross, death is no frightful leap in the dark, but is the entrance into a glorious new life. The Apostle Paul said: "For to me to live is Christ, and to die is gain. (Philippians 1:21) For the believer the brutal fact of death has been conquered by the historical resurrection of Jesus Christ. For the person who has turned from sin and has received Christ as Lord and Savior, death is not the end. For the believer there is hope beyond the grave. There is a future life. As the poet John Oxenham has written:

> God writes in characters too grand
> For our short sight to understand,
> We catch but broken strokes and try
> To fathom all the mystery
> Of withered hopes, of death, of like,
> The endless war, the useless strife—
> But there, with larger, clearer sight,
> We shall see this — God's way was right.

Billy Graham
(at President Johnson's funeral)

CROSSING THE BAR

Sunset and evening star,
    And one clear call for me,
And may there be no moaning of the bar,
    When I put out to sea.

But such a tide as moving seems asleep,
    Too full for sound and foam,
When that which drew from out the boundless deep
    Turns again home.

Twilight and evening bell,
    And after that the dark:
And may there be no sadness of farewell,
    When I embark;

For tho' from out our borne of time and place
    The flood may bear me far,
I hope to see my Pilot face to face
    When I have crossed the bar.

Alfred, Lord Tennyson

5.

When Doubts Threaten Your Faith and God Seems Far Away

"We lost everything," a husband and wife lamented after a devastating fire had burned their home to the ground and destroyed almost everything in it. "No, you're wrong," interjected a veteran fireman, who stood nearby wiping sweat and soot from his brow. "You lost your home and your belongings. But you have your children and each other—the important things."

Sometimes when we are surrounded by problems and our

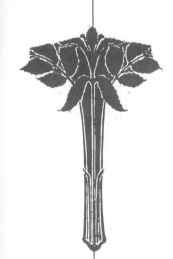

lives are in disarray, doubts can begin to creep insidiously into our lives. We forget to recognize our blessings, and God may seem far away. Through the ages, the Bible and other writings have affirmed the Lord's existence and His unfailing love for us.

Karl Barth, the famous Swiss theologian whose prolific prose on Christianity numbers many millions of words, was asked once to sum up his religious beliefs. He thought about the question for a moment, then answered, "Jesus loves me, this I know, for the Bible tells me so."

The most important part of our task will be to tell everyone who will listen that Jesus is the only answer to the problems that are disturbing the hearts of men and nations. We shall have the right to speak because we can tell from our experience that His light is more powerful than the deepest darkness . . . How wonderful that the reality of His presence is greater than the reality of the hell about us.

Betsie ten Boom (to her sister, Corrie)

Joyful, joyful, we adore Thee,
God of glory, Lord of love;
Hearts unfold like flowers before Thee,
Opening to the sun above.
Melt the clouds of sin and sadness,
Drive the dark of doubt away;
Giver of immortal gladness,
Fill us with the light of day.

Henry van Dyke   (hymn)

I believe in the Sun
    even when it is not shining.
I believe in Love
    even when I feel it not.
I believe in God
    even when He is silent.

Anonymous

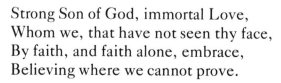

Once when I was going through a dark period I prayed and prayed, but the heavens seemed to be brass. I felt as though God had disappeared and that I was all alone with my trial and burden. It was a dark night for my soul. I wrote my mother about the experience, and will never forget her reply: "Son, there are many times when God withdraws to test your faith. He wants you to trust Him in the darkness. Now, Son, reach up by faith in the fog and you will find that His hand will be there." In tears I knelt by my bed and experienced an over-whelming sense of God's presence. Whether or not we sense and feel the presence of the Holy Spirit or one of the holy angels, by faith we are certain God will never leave us nor forsake us.

Billy Graham

Strong Son of God, immortal Love,
Whom we, that have not seen thy face,
By faith, and faith alone, embrace,
Believing where we cannot prove.

Alfred, Lord Tennyson (hymn)

For the Lord thy God is a merciful God. He will not forsake thee.

Deuteronomy 4 :31

81

He loves each one of us, as if there were only one of us.

Saint Augustine

Faith is the substance of things hoped for, the evidence of things not seen.

Hebrews 11 :1

I know the Bible
is inspired
because
it inspires me.

Dwight L. Moody

It takes a lot of courage to ask God through prayer when you know He will reply. Is God such a stranger that I hesitate to ask Him anything? It takes more faith to receive God's answer than to ask of Him in the first place.

Leonard G. Clough

"The wind bloweth where it listeth,
    but thou canst not tell..."
Who has seen the wind?
    Neither I nor you.
But when the leaves hang trembling,
    The wind is passing through.
Who has seen the wind?
    Neither you nor I.
But when the trees bow down their heads,
    The wind is passing by.

Christina Rossetti

Be still, and know that I am God.

Psalm 46 :10

O, Lord, thou hast searched me, and known me...
Whither shall I go from thy spirit?
  or whither shall I flee from thy presence?
If I ascend up into heaven, thou art there:
  if I make my bed in hell, behold, thou art there.
If I take the wings of the morning,
  and dwell in the uttermost parts of the sea:
Even there shall thy hand lead me,
  and thy right hand shall hold me.

Psalm 139 :1, 7-10

Simply trusting every day,
Trusting through a stormy way!
Even when my faith is small,
Trusting Jesus—that is all.

Ira D. Sankey (hymn)

Our Lord has written the promise of the Resurrection, not in books alone, but in every leaf in Springtime.

Martin Luther

George Mueller was the founder of a famous orphanage in Bristol, England. One of Mueller's operating principles was that this large institution would exist without fund drives or solicitations. They would, their director insisted, live on faith. Though the orphanage's resources were often low, somehow they always managed.

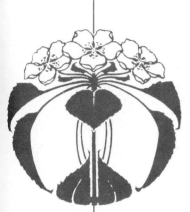

Once, shortly before dinnertime, an assistant came to Mueller and told him that there was no food in the kitchen. "The Lord will provide," Mueller answered. A half hour later, the man returned with the same concern. "Get the children ready for the meal," Mueller told him.

When they gathered at the table, there was nothing there but the utensils. "Now what do we do?" the distraught assistant whispered. "Say grace," Mueller answered, and he thanked God for supplying the orphanage's every need. As he finished, a truck pulled up into the driveway outside.It was full of bread sent by a baker. He'd had an oversupply and, for some unexplained reason, had asked a worker to deliver his extra loaves there.

Faith never
knows where it is being led, but it loves
and knows the One who is leading.

Oswald Chambers

I am not skilled to understand
What God hath willed, what God hath planned:
I only know at His right hand
Stands One who is my Savior.

I take Him at His word and deed:
"Christ died to save me," this I read;
And in my heart I find a need
Of Him to be my Savior.

That He should leave His place on high
And come for sinful man to die,
You count it strange? so once did I
Before I knew my Savior.

Dora Greenwell (hymn)

Jesus Christ will never strong-arm his way into your life.

Grady B. Wilson

God is He without whom one cannot live.

Leo Tolstoy

Doth not all nature around me praise God? If I were silent, I should be an exception to the universe. Doth not the thunder praise Him as it rolls like drums in the march of the God of armies? Do not the mountains praise Him when the woods upon their summits wave in adoration? Does not the lightning write His name in letters of fire? Hath not the whole earth a voice? And shall I, can I, silent be?

Charles H. Spurgeon

Lord, I believe: help thou mine unbelief.

Mark 19 :24

If you aren't as close to God as you once were, you can be very certain as to which one of you has moved.

Burton Hillis

A man can accept what Christ has done without knowing how it works; indeed, he certainly won't know how it works until he's accepted it.

C. S. Lewis

When we are faithful to keep ourselves in His holy presence and set Him always before us, . . . it begets in us a holy freedom and a familiarity with God.

Brother Lawrence

I KNOW THAT MY REDEEMER LIVETH

They asked me how I know it's true
That the Saviour lived and died . . .
And if I believe the story
That the Lord was crucified?
And I have so many answers
To prove His Holy Being,
Answers that are everywhere
Within the realm of seeing . . .
The leaves that fell at Autumn
And were buried in the sod
Now budding on the tree boughs
To lift their arms to God . . .
The flowers that were covered
And entombed beneath the snow
Pushing through the "darkness"
To bid the Spring "hello" . . .
On every side Great Nature
Retells the Easter Story—
So who am I to question
"The Resurrection Glory."

Helen Steiner Rice

God could have put his message for mankind in flaming letters of lightning across the sky. He could have had it sung by angels for the whole world to hear. Instead, he translated himself into his Son, who walked the hot, dusty roads of

Palestine. Today, again, God could translate his message into all the thousand of cultures and languages by running it through some gigantic computer. But he has chosen not to do so. He still chooses to communicate his truth through human personalities. He chooses to walk narrow paths of tropical jungles, hard sidewalks of concrete jungles, and grassy lawns of suburban jungles through translators like you and me, if we will take the risk of letting his treasure be carried to a lost and seeking world in the clay jars of our imperfect lives.

Leighton Ford

All I have seen teaches me to trust the Creator for all I have not seen.

Ralph Waldo Emerson

If thou canst believe, all things are possible to him that believeth.

Mark 9 :23

Blessed assurance, Jesus is mine!
O what a foretaste of glory divine!
Heir of salvation, purchase of God,
Born of His Spirit, washed in His Blood.

Fanny J. Crosby (hymn)

To seek the meaning of things and God's will does not spare us either from error or from doubt; nor does it solve all the mysteries of our destiny, all the insoluble problems which are sent us by any event of Nature or in our lives; nevertheless, it does give a new meaning to our lives.

Paul Tournier

To be certain of God means that we are uncertain in all our ways, we do not know what a day may 'bring forth. This is generally said with a sigh of sadness; it should be rather an expression of breathless expectation. We are uncertain of the next step, but we are certain of God. Immediately we abandon to God, and do the duty that lies nearest, He packs our lives with surprises all the time.

Oswald Chambers

His love for me is greater far
Than distance to a shining star,
Priceless as a golden treasure,
Scopeless and beyond all measure,
Deeper than the deepest sea,
Timeless as eternity.

Fred Bauer

Depend upon it, God's work done in God's way will never lack God's supplies.

J. Hudson Taylor

Either Jesus never was or he still is. As a typical product of these confused times, with a skeptical mind and a sensual disposition, diffidently and unworthily, but with the utmost certainty, I assert that he still is. If the story of Jesus had ended on Golgotha, it would indeed be of a Man Who Died, but as two thousand years later the Man's promise that *where two or three are gathered together in my name, there am I in the midst of them,* manifestly still holds, it is actually the story of a Man Who Lives.

Malcolm Muggeridge

When you read God's Word, you must constantly be saying to yourself, "It is
to me it is said, about me it is spoken."

Sören Kierkegaard

Lord, thou hast been our dwelling place
   in all generations.
Before the mountains were brought forth, or ever
   thou hadst formed the earth and the world,
   even from everlasting to everlasting,
   thou art God.
Thou turnest man to destruction; and sayest,
   Return, ye children of men.
For a thousand years in thy sight
are but as yesterday when it is past,
   and as a watch in the night.

Psalm 90 :1-4

Yesterday, today, forever, Jesus is the same.
All may change, but Jesus never! Glory to His Name!

Albert B. Simpson (hymn)

I never saw a moor,
I never saw the sea;
Yet know I how the heather looks,
And what a wave must be.

I never spoke with God
Nor visited in heaven;
Yet certain am I of the spot
As if the chart were given.

Emily Dickinson

Not what, but Whom, I do believe,
That, in my darkest hour of need,
Hath comfort that no mortal creed
To mortal man may give;
Not what, but Whom!
For Christ is more than all the creeds,
And His full life of gentle deeds
Shall all the creeds outlive.
Not what I do believe, but Whom!
Who walks beside me in the gloom?
Who shares the burden wearisome?
Who all the dim way doth illume,
And bids me look beyond the tomb
The larger life to live?
But whom!
Not what,
But Whom!

John Oxenham

The Bible is the one book to which any thoughtful man may go
with any honest question of life or destiny and find the answer
of God by honest searching.

John Ruskin

The principal part of faith is patience.

George Macdonald

Give us a pure heart that we may see Thee,
A humble heart that we may hear Thee,
A heart of love that we may serve Thee,
A heart of faith that we may live Thee.

Dag Hammarskjöld

Blessed are those who have not seen and yet believe.

John 20 :29

There is an ocean — cold water without motion. In this ocean, however, is the Gulf Stream, hot water flowing from the equator toward the Pole. Inquire of all scientists how it is physically imaginable that a stream of hot water flows between the waters of the ocean, which, so to speak, form its banks, the moving within the motionless, the hot within the cold. No scientist can explain it. Similarly, there is the God of love within the God of the forces of the universe—one with Him, and yet so totally different. We let ourselves be seized and carried away by that vital stream.

Albert Schweitzer

Earth changes, but thy soul and God stands sure:
    What entered into thee,
    That was, is, and shall be:
Time's wheel runs back or stops;
    Potter and clay endure.

Robert Browning

Immortal, invisible, God only wise
In light inaccessible hid from our eyes.
Most blessed, most glorious, the Ancient of Days,
Almighty, victorious, thy great Name we praise.

Great Father of glory, pure Father of light,
Thine angels adore thee, all veiling their sight;
All laud we would render; O help us to see
'Tis only the splendor of light hideth thee.

Walter C. Smith (hymn)

Whoso draws nigh to God one step
   through doubtings dim,
God will advance a mile
   in blazing light to him.

Anonymous

We know that all things work together for good to them that love God.

Romans 8 :28

I sought the Lord, and afterward I knew
He moved my soul to seek him, seeking me;
It was not I that found, O Savior true;
No, I was found of thee.

Thou didst reach forth thy hand and mine enfold;
I walked and sank not on the storm-vexed sea;
'Twas not so much that I on thee took hold
As thou, dear Lord, on me.

I find, I walk, I love, but oh, the whole
Of love is but my answer, Lord, to thee!
For thou wert long beforehand with my soul;
Always thou lovedst me.

Anonymous

Often has it happened to me to find, on awaking in the morning, a perfect army of doubts clamoring at my door for admittance. Nothing has seemed real, nothing has seemed true; and least of all had it seemed possible that I—miserable, wretched I—could be the object of the Lord's love, or care, or notice. If I only had been at liberty to let these doubts in, and invite them to take seats and make themselves at home, what a luxury I should many times have felt it to be! But years ago I made a pledge against doubting. I have never dared to admit the first doubt. At such times, therefore, I have been compelled to lift up the "shield of faith" the moment I have become conscious of these suggestions of doubt; and handing the whole army over to the Lord to conquer, I have begun to assert, over and over, my faith in Him, in the simple words, "God is my Father; I am His forgiven child; He does love me; Jesus saves me; Jesus saves me now!" The victory has always been complete.

Hannah Whitall Smith

TRUST THE GREAT ARTIST

Trust the Great Artist. He
Who paints the sky and sea
With shadowed blue, who clothes the land
In garb of green, and in the spring
Sets all earth blossoming—
He guides your destiny.

The magic hand
That colors dawn with flaming rose,
That ere the falling night,
For every soul's delight,
Pours out the steaming gold—
That hand too holds your life.

His grasp, amid the strife,
Would shape you to His will:
Let Him his wish fulfill.
What though the testings irk,
Fret not: mar not His work.
Trust the Great Artist, He
Who made the earth and sea.

Thomas Curtis Clark

Oh, I have heard a golden trumpet blowing
Under the night. Another warmth than blood
Has coursed, though briefly, through my intricate veins.
Some sky is in my breast where swings a hawk
Intemperate for immortalities
And unpersuaded by the show of death.
I am content with that I cannot prove.

William Alexander Percy

O Word of God incarnate,
O Wisdom from on high,
O Truth unchanged, unchanging,
O Light of our dark sky,
We praise thee for the radiance
That from the hallowed page,
A lantern to our footsteps,
Shines on from age to age.

William H. How

The more accurately we search into the human mind, the stronger traces we everywhere find of the wisdom of Him who made it.

Edmund Burke

I once saw a church that was really no more than a ceiling—here it was canvas, there it was metal. The people told me that once they had a beautiful brick church, but they were in a country where Christianity was not allowed, and someone had burned down the church.

I told them that I was so sorry they had lost their building, but they smiled. "God does not make mistakes. Some time ago," they said, "there was an earthquake on a Sunday morning. A thousand people were under this ceiling. Had we been in a brick building, many would have been injured, but this ceiling just quaked along with the earthquake, and no one was hurt."

Corrie ten Boom

Search the scriptures . . . which testifieth of me.

John 5:39

I know not what the future hath
   Of marvel or surprise,
Assured along that life and death
   His mercy underlies.

And if my heart and flesh are weak
   To bear an untired pain,
The bruised reed He will not break,
   But strengthen and sustain.

No offering of my own I have,
   Nor works my faith to prove;
I can but give the gifts He gave
   And plead His love for love.

And so beside the silent sea
   I wait the muffled oar;
No harm from Him can come to me
   On ocean or on shore.

I know not where His islands lift
   Their fronded palms in air;
I only know I cannot drift
   Beyond His love and care.

John Greenleaf Whittier

95

6.

When Illness Slows You Down

Writing in her autobiography, the late Helen Steiner Rice said, "While we all wonder why bad things have to happen to 'good people,' we also know that just being good and loving God and trying to serve Him does not guarantee us immunity from trouble, suffering, pain and sickness. But we must remember that 'God knows best'! And we can be sure that, while it is impossible for us to understand why things happen as they do, there is always a definite purpose

behind everything that happens to us, even though we may take long months or years to discover what the true purpose was. . . .

"My poem called 'Yesterday, Today and Tomorrow' has brought much comment from people who have received insight from it. To know there is no tomorrow, no yesterday but only the minute you are living in (and that minute has eternity in it) makes it possible to accept *the things that are happening to you."*

Yesterday's dead,
Tomorrow's unborn,
So there's nothing to fear
And nothing to mourn,
For all that is past
And all that has been
Can never return
To be lived once again—
And what lies ahead
Or the things that will be
Are still in GOD'S HANDS
So it is not up to me
To live in the future
That is God's great unknown,
For the past and the present
God claims for His own.
So all I need do
Is to live for TODAY
And trust God to show me
THE TRUTH AND THE WAY
For it's only the memory
Of things that have been
And expecting tomorrow
To bring trouble again
That fills my today,

Which God wants to bless,
With uncertain fears
And borrowed distress—
For all I need live for
Is this one little minute,
For life's HERE and NOW
And ETERNITY'S in it.

Keep these thoughts ever in mind; let them penetrate deep within your heart, for they will mean real life for you, and radiant health.

Proverbs 4 :21-22 (Living Bible)

When General William Booth, founder of the Salvation Army, was told that he was going blind and that doctors could do no more for him, he said, "God must know best. I have done what I could for Him and the people with my eyes. Now I shall do what I can for God and the people without my eyes."

The healing of His seamless dress
Is by our beds of pain;
We touch Him in life's throng and press,
And we are whole again.

John Greenleaf Whittier

Glorify God in your body, and in your spirit, which are God's.

I Corinthians 6 :20

Dr. S. W. Mitchell, a celebrated Philadelphia neurologist, had gone to bed after an exceptionally tiring day. Suddenly he was awakened by someone knocking on his door. Opening it he found a little girl, poorly dressed and deeply upset. She told him her mother was very sick, and asked him if he would please come with her. Though it was a bitterly cold, snowy night, and he was bone tired, Dr. Mitchell dressed and followed the girl. . . .

He found the mother desperately ill with pneumonia. After arranging for medical care, he complimented the sick woman on the intelligence and persistence of her little daughter. The woman looked at him strangely and then said, "My daughter died a month ago." She added, "Her shoes and coat are in the clothes closet there." Dr. Mitchell, amazed and perplexed, went to the closet and opened the door. There hung the very coat worn by the little girl who had brought him to tend her mother. It was warm and dry and could not possibly have been out in the wintry night.

Could the doctor have been called in the hour of desperate need by an angel who appeared as this woman's daughter? Was this the work of God's angels on behalf of the sick woman?

Billy Graham

If you live close to God
and His infinite grace,
You don't have to tell,
it shows on your face.

Anonymous

Jesus spoke, but he also healed. The two went together; they were the equipoise between loving God and loving one's neighbor—the two duties into which Jesus resolved all that the Law laid down and the prophets had proclaimed. Even in the

Garden of Gethsemane he healed, restoring the man's ear that Peter had impulsively hacked off with his sword. For that matter, even on the Cross he offered healing words to the penitent thief crucified beside him, making a rendezvous with him in paradise. Jesus never for one moment forgot our human need for bodies and minds in working order; for eyes that truly see and ears that truly hear. His compassion for the maimed, whether they were physically, mentally or spiritually disabled, was fathomless.

Malcolm Muggeridge

Beloved, I wish above all things that thou mayst prosper and be in health, even as thy soul prospereth.

III John 1 :2

My life is but a weaving
   Between my God and me;
I do not choose the colors
   He weaveth steadily.
Sometimes He weaveth sorrow,
   And I in foolish pride
Forget He sees the upper
   And I the underside.

Not till the loom is silent
   And the shuttles cease to fly
Will God unroll the canvas
   And explain the reason why
The dark threads are as needed
   In the skillful Weaver's hand
As the threads of gold and silver
   In the pattern He has planned.

Author unknown

"For I will restore health unto thee, and I will heal thee of thy wounds, saith the Lord.

Jeremiah 30 :17

I spent the whole of August suffering from a not dangerous but intensely painful illness. During the weeks that I was completely flattened I received a whole raft of blessings, some of them apparent from the start, some to become clear only later. The immediate grace I received was of realizing at all times that the pain was an opportunity and had a reason even though I didn't know what the reason was. I tried to explain to Ned how comforting it was to feel that your suffering could be made to work for you or for others.

"Do you mean you're being punished or something?" he asked.

No, I felt simply that I was being handed a chance to suffer with Christ in an infinitesimal way, to give Him my own inadequate return for all the suffering He endured for me; for all of us. . . .

That night I woke up after an hour or two of sleep, and found myself lying on my right side in searing pain. I knew that in spite of the room's being dark, I was lying in a flow of strong light, that God was near to me and that this was His light. I felt wildly happy—not peaceful—completely elated. In a flash I knew with no difficulty at all the answer to the "Why?" of pain. I heard no voices, saw no visions, but as clearly as spoken words I heard the answer to that age-old question: "Why me?" — "Because I love you very much."

Naomi Burton

The chamber of sickness is the chapel of devotion.

Anonymous

And he said unto me, My grace is sufficient for thee: for my strength is made perfect in weakness. Most gladly therefore will I rather glory in my infirmities, that the power of Christ may rest upon me.

II Corinthians 12 :9

Though I am weak,
   yet God, when prayed,
Cannot withhold
   His conquering aid.

Ralph Waldo Emerson

The Lord sustains him on his sickbed; in his illness thou healest all his infirmities.

Psalm 41 :3 (RSV)

What we suffer now is nothing compared to the glory he will give us later. For all creation is waiting patiently and hopefully for that future day when God will resurrect his children. For on that day thorns and thistles, sin, death, and decay—the things that overcame the world against its will at God's command— will all disappear, and the world around us will share in the glorious freedom from sin which God's children enjoy.

For we know that even the things of nature, like animals and plants, suffer in sickness and death as they await this great event. And even we Christians, although we have the Holy spirit within us as a foretaste of future glory, also groan to be released from pain and suffering. We, too, wait anxiously for that day when God will give us our full rights as his children, including the new bodies he has promised us—bodies that will never be sick again and will never die.

And in the same way—by our faith—the Holy Spirit helps us

with our daily problems and in our praying. For we don't even know what we should pray for, nor how to pray as we should; but the Holy Spirit prays for us with such feeling that it cannot be expressed in words. And the Father who knows all hearts knows, of course, what the Spirit is saying as he pleads for us in harmony with God's own will. And we know that all that happens to us is working for our good if we love God and are fitting into his plans.

Romans 8 :18-28 (Living Bible)

O what a happy soul am I!
Although I cannot see,
I am resolved that in this world
Contented I will be;
How many blessings I enjoy
That other people don't!
To weep, and sigh because I'm blind,
I cannot, and I won't.

Fanny Crosby

Then one day I found somewhere, on a page I have since forgotten, three words which had greater power than even the doctor's words. When I began to feel the horror coming on, I said to myself, "God within me . . . God within me." While I was saying those three words I felt and I knew that I was no longer alone. All of a sudden, because of those three words, I could walk along the street without fear. Saying "God within me" brought me an inrush of quietness and sweetness, a feeling inside me of dignity and wholeness which was not me at all, but something greater than I was, against which the horrors were powerless.

Katharine Butler Hathaway

Is there any sick among you? let him call for the elders of the church; and let them pray over him, anointing him with oil in the name of the Lord:

And the prayer of faith shall save the sick, and the Lord shall raise him up.

James 5:14-15

When the blind suppliant in the way,
 By friendly hands to Jesus led,
Prayed to behold the light of day,
 "Receive thy sight," the Saviour said.

At once he saw the pleasant rays
 That lit the glorious firmament;
And, with firm step and words of praise,.
 He followed where the Master went.

Look down in pity, Lord, we pray,
 On eyes oppressed by mortal night,
And touch the darkened lids and say,
 The gracious words, "Receive thy sight."

Then, in clear daylight, shall we see
 Where walked the sinless Son of God;
And, aided by new strength from Thee,
 Press onward in the path He trod.

William Cullen Bryant

I remember one October night visiting a friend who was lying very sick. There was a full moon that night; and as I walked down the village street on my sad mission I felt the silvery beauty of it quiet my heart. The world lay lustrous. There was no scrawny bush nor ugly clod that was not transfigured in that glory. A little breeze over the brimming salt tide brought aromatic marshy odors. It seemed to me that some

power was trying to make beauty take away my sadness. I found my friend not less aware than I was of the beauty of the night. He could look from his window and see the argent glamour of it all: how it flooded the gleaming tide with celestial lights; how it ran long white lances through the swarthy cedars; how it tinged with soft radiance the locusts and the mimosas. He felt the breeze too, and delighted in the odors that brought of the happy world beyond his window.

As I sat beside him, a mockingbird began to sing in the moonlight, chanting divinely. I know the song reached our spirits. On the table by the bed were all the necessities for a sick man; but he had small comfort from them. But the moonlight, and the hale fragrances, and the wild song of the bird— these brought peace to his heart.

Long afterward he said to me, "Do you remember that night? I thought it would be my last. But from the time the birdsong came through that window I felt that I would get well. I don't talk much about these things, but I felt that all that beauty and peace were really the love of God. I guess He does not love us with words: He loves us by giving us everything we need—in every way."

Archibald Rutledge

A bodily disease which we look upon as whole and entire within itself, may, after all, be but a symptom of some ailment in the spiritual part.

Nathaniel Hawthorne

"I am the Lord that healeth thee.

Exodus 15 :26

Send down thy winged angel, God!
    Amidst this night so wild;
And bid him come where now we watch,
    And breathe upon our child!

She lies upon her pillow, pale,
    And moans within her sleep,
Or wakeneth with a patient smile,
    And striveth *not* to weep!

How gentle and how good a child
    She is, we know too well,
And dearer to her parents' heart
    Than our weak words can tell.

We love,—we watch throughout the night,
    To aid, when need may be;
We hope,—and have despaired, at times;
    But *now* we turn to Thee!

Send down thy sweet-souled angel, God!
    Amidst the darkness wild,
And bid him soothe our souls to-night,
    And heal our gentle child!

Barry Cornwall

"And Jesus went about all Galilee, healing all manner of sickness and all manner of disease among the people."

Matthew 4 :23

Is not this the fast that I choose:
    to loose the bonds of wickedness
Then shall your light break forth like the dawn,
    and your healing shall spring up speedily.

Isaiah 58 :8 (RSV)

A man's spirit will endure sickness; but a broken spirit who can bear?

Proverbs 18:14 (RSV)

Precious Lord, take my hand,
Lead me on, help me stand;
I am tired, I am weak, I am worn;
Thru the storm, thru the night,
Lead me on to the light,
Take my hand, precious Lord, lead me home.

Thomas A. Dorsey   (hymn)

I met a woman in Russia who had multiple sclerosis. Her feet and hands were paralyzed except for one finger. With that one finger she typed out Bible texts and inspirational books.

This woman's husband bound her typewritten messages together into books which then went from one person to another. She did this work until the day she died. She is now with the Lord. How happy she is! And I am sure that she has heard from many there who have read her literature, "It was you who invited me here." Do not say you are not healthy or strong enough—you have more than one finger to use for God's work!

Corrie ten Boom

As Jesus and the disciples were going to the rabbi's home, a woman who had been sick for twelve years with internal bleeding came up behind him and touched a tassel of his robe, for she thought, "If I only touch him, I will be healed."

Jesus turned around and spoke to her. "Daughter," he said "all is well! Your faith has healed you." And the woman was well from that moment.

Matthew 9:19-22 (Living Bible)

110

In the hour of trial,
Jesus, plead for me,
Lest by base denial
I depart from thee;
When thou seest me waver,
With a look recall,
Nor for fear or favor
Suffer me to fall.

Should thy mercy send me
Sorrow, toil or woe,
Or should pain attend me
On my path below,
Grant that I may never
Fail thy hand to see;
Grant that I may ever
Cast my care on thee.
James Montgomery (hymn)

As the sun went down that evening, all the villagers who had any sick people in their homes, no matter what their diseases were, brought them to Jesus: and the touch of his hands healed every one!

Luke: 4:40 (Living Bible)

Among the students at a college was a young man on crutches. Although not a particularly handsome fellow, he had a talent for friendliness and optimism, and he gained high scholastic honors and earned the respect of his classmates. One day a classmate asked him what had caused him to become so badly crippled.

"Infantile paralysis," said the young man on crutches.

"With misfortune like that," said his friend, "how can you face the world so confidently and happily?"

"Because," replied the polio victim, "the disease never reached my heart."

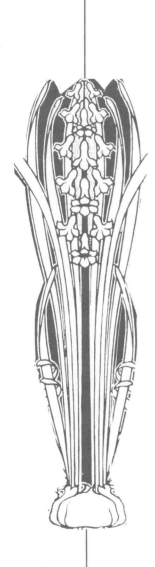

Sometimes a light surprises
    The Christian while he sings;
It is the Lord who rises
    With healing in his wings.
When comforts are declining
    He grants the soul again
A season of clear shining,
    To cheer it after rain.

William Cowper

O Lord my God, I cried unto thee, and thou hast healed me.

Psalm 30 :2

We never find ideal conditions of life and work. We always think that if only things were different, we could really show what we were capable of . . . This is true of all kinds of afflictions. Consider two of my patients. One is impatient at the time he is wasting. The other writes to me: "How nice it is to have time to spare, even if it is only the time to be ill." For illness relieves you of all other duties. One patient wears himself out in revolt and in insoluable arguments in the problem of evil; another writes: "I have learned to go beyond the question of 'why illness?' to that of 'what can I learn from my illness?'" One person learns patience, understanding, and compassion for others; another becomes unbearable.

Paul Tournier

God be merciful unto us, and bless us;
and cause his face to shine upon us;
That thy way may be known upon earth,
thy saving health among all nations.

Psalm 67 : 1, 2

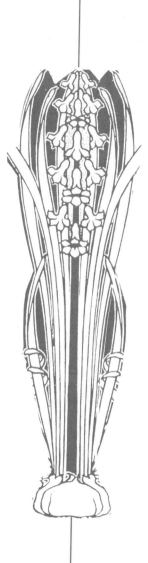

In 1973 Orville Kelly learned that he was terminally ill with cancer. For a while this 42-year-old man stood mute in shock, unable to communicate with anyone about the fear and loneliness and bitterness that pulsed inside him. He did ask God to perform a miracle and heal him, but that didn't happen. Then he prayed to die—quickly. Finally, when he was at the bottom of his despair, he relinquished his problem to God. "Do with me what You will," he prayed. At that point God spoke to him:

You are no different from anyone else, Orville. Everyone is dying. Man was born to die. But he also was born to live— fully, enthusiastically, abundantly. No one on earth is promised more than one day of life at a time. You have today. Make today count.

Orville Kelly took the message to heart. He reached out to other terminally ill people who needed someone with whom to share their burdens and faith. He organized a local group of cancer sufferers. They named it "Make Today Count," and today it is a national organization with chapters around the country. Orville Kelly has gone home to be with the Lord, but because he prayed about his illness and acted upon the guidance he received from God, others have found the courage and strength to live triumphantly and to make each day count.

I wish you could convince yourself that God is often nearer to us, and more effectively present with us, in sickness than in health.

Brother Lawrence

The hearing ear and the seeing eye, the Lord hath made even both of them.

Proverbs 20 :12

A merry heart doeth good like a medicine.

Proverb 17:22

There is no music in a "rest," but there is the making of music in it. In our whole life melody, the music is broken off here and there by "rests" and we foolishly think we have come to the end of the tune. God sends a time of forced leisure, sickness, disappointed plans, frustrated efforts that makes a sudden pause in the choral hymn of our lives, and we lament that our voice must be silent and our part missing in the music which ever goes up to the ear of the Creator. How does the musician read the rest? See him beat the time with unvarying count and catch up the next note true and steady as if no breaking place had come in between. Not without design does God write the music of our lives. But be it ours to learn the time and not be dismayed at the "rests." They are not to be slurred over, not to be omitted, nor to destroy the melody, nor to change the keynote. If we look up, God Himself will beat the time for us. With the eye on Him, we shall strike the next note full and clear.

John Ruskin

7.

When You Need Life-restoring Forgiveness

And the scribes and Pharisees brought unto him a woman taken in adultery; and when they had set her in the midst, they said unto him, Master, this woman was taken in adultery, in the very act. Now Moses in the law commanded us, that such should be stoned; but what sayst thou?

This they said, tempting him, that they might have to accuse him. But Jesus stooped down, and with his finger wrote on the ground as though he heard them not. So when they continued asking him, he lifted up himself, and said

unto them, He that is without sin among you, let him first cast a stone at her. And again, he stooped down, and wrote on the ground. And they which heard it, being convicted by their own conscience, went out one by one, beginning at the eldest, even unto the last; and Jesus was left alone, and the woman standing in the midst.

When Jesus had lifted up himself, and saw none but the woman he said unto her, Woman, where are those thine accusers? hath no man condemned thee? She said, No man, Lord. And Jesus said unto her, Neither do I condemn thee: go, and sin no more.

John 8 : 3-11

Dear Father, I believe that Jesus Christ is Your only begotten Son, and that He became a human being, shed His blood and died on the cross to clean away my sin that was separating me from You. I believe that He rose from the dead, physically, to give me new life. Lord Jesus, I invite You to come into my heart. I accept You as my Savior and Lord. I confess my sins, and ask You to wash them away. I believe that You have come and are living in me right now. Thank you, Jesus! Amen.

Dennis and Rita Bennett

Just as I am, Thou wilt receive,
Wilt welcome, pardon, cleanse, relieve;
Because Thy promise I believe,
O Lamb of God, I come! I come!

Charlotte Elliott (hymn)

The way to be saved is not to delay, but to come and take.

Dwight L. Moody

For by grace are ye saved through faith; and that not of your-selves: it is the gift of God: not of works, lest any man should boast.

Ephesians 2 :8-9

God dropped a spark down into everyone,
    And if we find and fan it to a blaze,
It'll spring up and glow, like—like the sun,
    And light the wandering out of stony ways.

John Masefield

While working on his painting "The Last Supper," Leonardo da Vinci argued violently with a friend. Both men used bitter words, and they parted in anger. Da Vinci returned to his canvas, began to work on the face of Jesus, but soon quit when he discovered that he was doing poorly. The argument had so unnerved him that he was too upset to continue. Instead, he went to his friend's house to ask his forgiveness. Then he returned to work and was able to continue working on Christ's face.

Jesus my Lord will love me forever,
From Him no power of evil can sever,
He gave His life to ransom my soul,
Now I belong to Him;

    Now I belong to Jesus,
    Jesus belongs to me,

117

Not for the years of time alone,
But for eternity.

Once I was lost in sin's degradation,
Jesus came down to bring me salvation,
Lifted me up from sorrow and shame,
Now I belong to Him:

Joy floods my soul for Jesus has saved me,
Freed me from sin that long had enslaved me,
His precious blood He gave to redeem,
Now I belong to Him.

Norman J. Clayton (hymn)

When a spaceship returns from an orbital flight there is a blackout period of about four minutes when all communications are broken. This is due to the intense heat generated by re-entry into the earth's atmosphere. The Bible teaches that man is in a state of spiritual blackout. Communication between God and man is broken.

If the television set in your house is cold, dark and lifeless, that is not the fault of the TV. You must turn it on and tune in. God, too, is sending forth his message of love, but we must be willing to receive it.

Ralph S. Bell

Life that ever needs forgiveness has for its first duty to forgive.

Edward Bulwer-Lytton

If we confess our sins, he is faithful and just to forgive us our sins, and to cleanse us from all unrighteousness.

I John 1:9

I gave up Christianity at about fourteen. Came back to it when getting on for thirty. It was not an emotional conversion: almost purely philosophical. I didn't want to. I'm not in the least the religious type. I want to be let alone, to feel I'm my own master; but since the facts seemed to be just the opposite I had to give in.

C. S. Lewis

Before man can live rightly with others, he must first get right with God.

Charles L. Allen

I went very unwillingly to a society in Aldersgate Street, here one was reading Luther's preface to the *Epistle to the Romans.* While he was describing the change which God makes in the heart through faith in Christ, I felt my heart strangely warmed. I felt I did trust in Christ, Christ alone for salvation; and an assurance was given me that He had taken away *my* sins, even *mine,* and saved *me* from the law of sin and death.

John Wesley

When I survey the wondrous cross
On which the Prince of glory died,
My richest gain I count but loss,
And pour contempt on all my pride.

Forbid it, Lord, that I should boast,
Save in the death of Christ my God;
All the vain things that charm me most,
I sacrifice them to His blood.

See, from His head, His hands, His feet,
Sorrow and love flow mingled down:

Did e'er such love and sorrow meet,
Or thorns compose so rich a crown?

Were the whole realm of nature mine,
That were a present far too small;
Love so amazing, so divine,
Demands my soul, my life, my all.

Isaac Watts (hymn)

THE INCIDENT IN THE BUS STATION

It has always been hard for me to start a conversation with strangers about the Lord. I have found, though, that if I am reading the Bible, people often approach me. One day last fall as I was returning from helping my daughter with her new baby son, I had a two-hour wait between buses in Kansas City. I looked around at my fellow travelers in the depot and prayed that if anyone was there who needed to be told about the Lord, he would show me.

People milled about the room. An old man was asleep on a hard bench. A young mother and father wearily tried to keep two lively tots close to them and at the same time to soothe a fretful, tired baby. A group of boys in uniform talked quietly in one corner. Several other young people were waiting—office workers and students going home for the weekend.

A boy in a rumpled shirt and blue jeans hesitated, then sat down close to me. He seemed quite young, probably 16 or 17. He was nervous. He kept shifting his position, shuffling his feet, and drumming with tense, restless fingers. His face was clouded and drawn, very unlike the eager, glad faces of most of the other young people.

"That's a Bible, isn't it?" he asked, abruptly. "We used to read it lots at home. My mother would say that it could answer any problem you had in your life."

"Yes." I spoke thoughtfully. "I'm sure that she is right. It can solve our problems if we use it in the right way, praying and searching in it for God's will as it applies to us."

We sat silently for a while. Inwardly I prayed that I would say the right words. I felt that he surely had a deep need for help.

"When I was little, Mom used to take us to Sunday School," he mused. "And Dad would go. But then my mother got a job. Lots of Sundays now she has to work, and when she doesn't there is all the catching up to do at home."

"Do you have brothers and sisters? Maybe you could all do a little work to help her," I ventured. "Then you'd be able to go to church together again."

His jaw hardened.

"Helping her wouldn't change things. She just wants us to stay out of the way. And that's what I'm doing. I don't live there any more, and right here in my pocket I have a ticket that will take me a thousand miles away from here."

His story came pouring out. During the past summer he had found work too. It was a good job, so with his fine salary he bought himself a nice car on time payments. But when he returned to school, he couldn't work enough hours to meet the car payments as they came due.

"They wouldn't help me," he complained, close to tears. "My dad said I had to get rid of the car. He bawled me out because my grades were falling. Mom kept nagging me and nagging me for putting money into car repair. They said I had to sell it, use the money to buy clothes and books and pay school expenses. We had a big quarrel. I just moved out and quit school.

"Boy, I guess they'd really laugh if they kept track of me and knew how things have gone for me since then. They'd really be tickled.It was just like they said, because I lost the car anyway. I couldn't find work enough to keep it. I can't even pay for my room and board," he confessed, painfully.

"Oh, they wouldn't be happy at all," I insisted. "I know they'd be sorry that you had been so disappointed. I know they would want you to come right back home and get into school

again and finish your education!"

He laughed, bitterly, shortly.

"You just don't know them!"

He wasn't believing me; I was losing him, I knew. Suddenly I remembered something. I held up the Bible in my hands. "Say, there's a story just about like yours right here in the Bible." Hastily I leafed over to the parable of the prodigal son. He listened closely as I read it, and tears glistened in his eyes when I had finished.

"Uh-uh," he shook his head. "They wouldn't be about to kill the 'fatted calf' for me. I don't think I'd even rate a hamburger if I went home!" He tried to laugh lightly.

I told him of the deeper meaning of the story of the prodigal son. I explained how we are all prodigal sons of God, separated from him by our sins. I told him how we can repent our sins and surrender ourselves completely to Jesus Christ, receiving salvation and new life. Going through the Bible, I showed him the tremendous promises in John 1:12, 5:24; Romans 6:23, and Revelation 3:20.

"Can I do this right now, right here?" he asked. "Yes, you can," I said. Holding my Bible, he prayed, asking God's forgiveness for his sins, freely accepting Jesus as his Savior.

He looked up with a new, wonderful joy in his eyes.

"Now I have to do something else," he told me. "You see, I met these fellows. I think they are pretty wild. I was going out West to join them. They said we'd do real well together, but I don't know what they had in mind. Well, I think I'd better cash in my ticket. If I get out early in the morning and try hard I can find something to make my living."

"Yes, you could," I said. "But first, go call your parents. Let them know of the things that have happened to you. At least you should let them know that you are safe, so they won't worry."

"No, they wouldn't care. It doesn't make any difference to them."

"Please call them," I urged. "Remember the story in the

Bible. Think of that father and son."

Slowly he rose and I went with him to a phone booth. He dropped in a coin and dialed.

"Hello? Mom?" he choked, hoarsely. "This is Tim."

He didn't have to say more. I could hear his mother's excited, thankful voice, her tearful exclamations as she pleaded with him to tell her where he was, to let her come after him. Then a deeper voice was on the phone. Tim's face began to glow like a rising sun.

He turned to me.

"They do want me," he exclaimed. "I'm to wait right here. They are coming for me. What do you know!"

Very soon a car drove up. Children piled out to run to Tim and swarm all around him. A woman enveloped him in welcoming arms. His father grabbed the boy's suitcase and his arm to led him to the car. Tim came back to me just for a moment.

"Thank you for reading me the story," he said. "Thanks for telling me about it. I'm going to get a Bible and study it. I'll tell my folks and my friends how I found Jesus in it."

I stood alone until my bus was called. Joining the slowly moving line boarding it, I tightened my clasp on my Bible. I'd open it when I sat down inside. For as shy as I was, there might be another soul there who was badly in need, and wanting to begin a conversation about the Lord.

Lucille Campbell

Therefore if any man be in Christ, he is a new creature; old things are passed away; behold, all things are become new.

II Corinthians 5:17

God's forgiveness is not just a casual statement; it is the complete blotting out of all the dirt and degradation of our past, present and future. The only reason our sins can be forgiven is

because Jesus Christ paid their full penalty on the cross. ... God's goodness in forgiving us goes even farther when we realize that when we are converted we are also declared just— which means that in God's sight we are without guilt, clothed forever with Christ's righteousness.

Billy Graham

Thou has made us for Thyself and our hearts are restless until they rest in Thee.

St. Augustine

There is joy in the presence of the angels of God over one sinner that repenteth.

Luke 15 :10

I MET THE MASTER

I had walked life's way with an easy tread,
Had followed where comforts and pleasures led,
Until one day in a quiet place
I met the Master face to face.

With station and rank and wealth for my goal,
Much thought for my body but none for my soul,
I had entered to win in life's mad race,
When I met the Master face to face.

I met him and knew Him and blushed to see
That His eyes full of sorrow were fixed on me,
And I faltered and fell at His feet that day
While my castles melted and vanished away.

Melted and vanished, and in their place
Naught else did I see but the Master's face;
And I cried aloud, 'Oh, make me meet
To follow the steps of Thy wounded feet.'

My thought is now for the souls of men;
I have lost my life to find it again,
E'er since one day in a quiet place
I met the Master face to face.

Author Unknown

WHY SHOULD HE DIE FOR SUCH AS I

In everything both great and small
We see the hand of God in all,
And in the miracles of Spring
When everywhere in everything
His handiwork is all around
And every lovely sight and sound
Proclaims the God of earth and sky
I ask myself "just who am I"
That God should send His only Son
That my salvation should be won
Upon a cross by a sinless man
To bring fulfillment to God's plan—
For Jesus suffered, bled and died
That sinners might be sanctified,
And to grant God's children such as I
Eternal life in that home on high.

Helen Steiner Rice

125

O Love that will not let me go,
I rest my weary soul in Thee;
I give Thee back the life I owe,
That in Thine ocean depths its flow
May richer, fuller be.

O Light that followest all my way,
I yield my flickering torch to Thee;
My heart restores its borrowed ray,
That in Thy sunshine's blaze its day
May brighter, fairer be.

O Joy that seekest me through pain,
I cannot close my heart to Thee;
I trace the rainbow through the rain,
And feel the promise is not vain
That morn shall tearless be.

O Cross that liftest up my head,
I dare not ask to fly from Thee;
I lay in dust life's glory dead,
And from the ground there blossoms red,
Life that shall endless be.

George Matheson (hymn)

I think of the heart as a household, one with many rooms.... The more we love, the more room there is to love. I believe that when the Creator built into our beings the quality which enables us to love, He created us with an infinite capacity to embrace. We were intended to be loving creatures. He wanted us to have open hearts—nonprejudiced, nonpreferential, nondiscriminatory hearts. But His original design was turned topsy-turvy. Sin entered the creation, the creature . . . We are consequently the possessors of mean rooms—damp basements, narrow hallways, cramped spaces . . . The windows are shuttered, the blinds drawn. Dust is accumulating. The doors have been padlocked . . . Fortunately, our Creator in His great love has crafted a key that unlocks our fortified towers. It is a master key that opens all rooms, turns all rusty tumblers . . . The key that opens the door to the locked rooms of our hearts is called forgiveness.

Karen Burton Mains

Christians aren't perfect, just forgiven.

Unknown Author

If Christ is born a thousand times in Bethlehem and not in thee, then art thou lost for ever.

Angelus Silesius

I dreamed God came the other night,
And Heaven's gates swung wide.
With kindly grace an angel
Welcomed me inside,
And there to my astonishment
Stood folks I'd known on earth:
Some I'd judged and labeled
"Unfit, of little worth."
Angry words rose to my lips
But never were set free,
For every face showed stunned surprise—
None there expected me!

Anonymous

Turn to me and be saved, all the ends of the earth! For I am God, and there is no other.

Isaiah 45 :22 (RSV)

It's not in falling we fail,
Not in failing we fall.
Our faults admitted, pale,
The Lord forgives them all.

Fred Bauer

There is a story about the wife of one of Cyrus's generals who was charged with treachery against the king. She was called before Cyrus and after the trial condemned to die.

Her husband, who did not realize what had taken place, was apprised of it and came hurrying in. When he heard the sentence condemning his wife to death, he threw himself prostrate before the king and said, "O Sire, take my life instead of hers. Let me die in her place!" Cyrus was so touched that he said, "Love like that must not be spoiled by death," and he gave them back to each other and let the wife go free.

As they walked happily away the husband said, "Did you notice how kindly the king looked upon us when he gave you a free pardon?"

"I had no eyes for the king," she said. "I saw only the man who was willing to die for me."

H. A. Ironside

Beneath the cross of Jesus
I fain would take my stand,
The shadow of a mighty rock
Within a weary land;
A home within the wilderness,
A rest upon the way,
From the burning of the noontide heat
And the burden of the day.

Upon that cross of Jesus
Mine eye at times can see

The very dying form of One
Who suffered there for me;
And from my smitten heart with tears
Two wonders I confess—
The wonders of His glorious love
And my unworthiness.

I take, O cross, thy shadow
For my abiding place;
I ask no other sunshine than
The sunshine of His face;
Content to let the world go by,
To know no gain nor loss,
My sinful self my only shame,
My glory all the cross.

Elizabeth C. Clephane (hymn)

Up from the grave He arose,
With a mighty triumph o'er His foes;
He arose a victor from the dark domain,
And He lives forever with His saints to reign;
He arose! He arose! Hallelujah! Christ arose!

Robert Lowry (hymn)

He taught me all the mercy,
For he show'd me all the sin.
Now, tho' my lamp was lighted late,
There's One will let me in.

Alfred, Lord Tennyson

Often as I let my mind wander back to the great storms and blizzards that we went through on my ranches, I recall scenes full of pathos and power. Again and again I would come home to our humble cottage with two or three tiny, forlorn, cold lambs bundled up within the generous folds of my big, rough wool jacket. Outside hail, sleet, snow and chilling rain would be lashing my face and body. But within my arms, the lambs were safe and sure of survival. Part of the great compensation for enduring the blizzards. . . was to pick up lost lambs. And as I picked them up I realized in truth I was taking up my own life again in them. . . . It is as I am found in Him that He, too, revels and rejoices in my being found. No wonder there is such rejoicing in heaven over one lost soul who is brought home.

Phillip Keller

Sing, oh, sing of my Redeemer,
With His blood He purchased me,
On the cross He sealed my pardon,
Paid the debt, and made me free.

Philip P. Bliss (hymn)

I am here to pray that God will take you into his own workmanship, create you anew in Christ Jesus, give you to feel his Spirit's work on your heart, and make you his child. Don't say it cannot be. Don't say it shall not be. Don't say it is too late. Don't say it is for others but not for you. Turn this text into a prayer. Say, "Lord God, let me know what it is for you to work in me. Make me a new creature."

George Whitefield

Teach me to feel another's woe,
To hide the fault I see;
That mercy I to others show,
That mercy show to me.

Alexander Pope

8.

When Loneliness Engulfs You

One night a man dreamed that he was walking along a moonlit beach with the Lord. Across the sky flashed scenes from his life. In each scene, he often noticed two sets of footprints in the sand—one belonging to him, and the other to the Lord.

After the last scene of his life had flashed before him, he looked back at all the footprints in the sand. He noticed that many times along the path of his life there was only one set of prints. Strange, he thought; that single set of footprints

coincided with the lowest and saddest times in his life.

It bothered him considerably, so he decided to ask the Lord about it. "Lord, you said that once I decided to follow you, you'd walk with me all the way. But I've noticed that during the most troublesome times in my life, there was only one set of footprints. Why did you leave me alone when I needed you the most?"

The Lord replied, "My precious child, I love you and would never break my promise. I have never left you nor will I ever. During your times of trial and sorrow, when you saw only one set of footprints, it was then that I was carrying you."

OPEN MY EYES

God open my eyes
   so I may see
And feel Your presence
   close to me...
Give me strength
   for my stumbling feet
As I battle the crowd
   on life's busy street,
And widen the vision
   of my unseeing eyes
So in passing faces
   I'll recognize
Not just a stranger,
   unloved and unknown,
But a friend with a heart
   that is much like my own...

Give me perception
    to make me aware
That scattered profusely
    on life's thoroughfare
Are the best GIFTS of GOD
    that we daily pass by
As we look at the world
    with an UNSEEING EYE.

Helen Steiner Rice

He shall give you another Comforter; that he may abide with you for ever.

John 14 :16

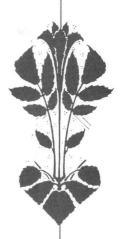

SANCTUARY

'Mid all the traffic of the ways,
Turmoils without, within,
Make in my heart a quiet place,
And come and dwell therein:

A little shrine of quietness,
All sacred to Thyself,
Where Thou shalt all my soul possess,
And I may find myself:

A little shelter from life's stress,
Where I may lay me prone,
And bare my soul in lowliness
And know as I am known:

A little place of mystic grace,
Of self and sin swept bare,
Where I may look into Thy face,
And talk with Thee in prayer.

John Oxenham

There is a place of quiet rest
Near to the heart of God,
A place where sin cannot molest,
Near to the heart of God.

Cleland B. McAfee (hymn)

'Lo, I am with you always, even unto the end of the world.

Matthew 28:20

Thou layest Thy hand on the fluttering heart
And sayest, "Be still!"
The Shadow and silence are only a part
    Of Thy sweet will.
Thy presence is with me, and where Thou art
    I fear no ill.

Frances Ridley Havergal

In our church a circle of older women had been meeting for fifteen years and was showing some interest in covenant groups, although it was mostly curiosity and with no little criticism and reservation. They asked me a lot of questions about the subject as we met one day for the monthly Bible study. Having heard several answers, they generally agreed that this kind of group was not for them.

"Why not?" I asked.

"I can't speak for the rest of us," one woman said, "but in my case, I was brought up to keep my problems to myself. To open up my life in such a way would be—well, it would be a sign of weakness."

"It's been the same with me," another woman said. "After all, who cares about our problems? Oh, perhaps we might discuss something personal with a few close friends, but, even then, that isn't why we get together."

The other women agreed. They all had been brought up in much the same way.

"How do you feel about that?" I asked.

"About what?"

"About that kind of cultural conditioning? That stiff-upper-lip, don-t-wear-your-heart-on-your-sleeve, I- can-take-care-of-myself sort of thing?"

I thought perhaps I had probed a little too far and expected a sharp retort. But the woman who had spoken first said, "It leaves me very lonely."

Her openness did something to the others, and within a few minutes they were sharing their inner struggles. One woman said, "I wish I could talk over some of these things with somebody." Another said, "I've carried some burdens for years, and nobody ever knew about them."

"Tell me," I asked the first woman, "what would be necessary before you could talk about your hopes and disappointments — your deepest feelings — with another person?"

She thought for a moment, then stated it beautifully: "I think I would have to be able to trust the other person." They all nodded in agreement.

Then a woman who had recently lost her husband began to talk about her loneliness, and it was interesting to see the reactions of the others as she began to reveal her emotional pain. One or two were embarrassed by it; the others moved their chairs close to her. As she began to cry, a few put their arms around her.

These women had been meeting in a church for fifteen years and only now were they beginning to include each other in their lives. In one hour they were well on their way to becoming a loving, caring family of human beings who could actually feel God's love moving through them.

Louis H. Evans, Jr.

The Lord watch between me and thee, when we are absent one from another.

Genesis 31 :49

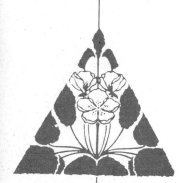

O Thou who dry'st the mourner's tear!
   How dark this world would be,
If, when deceived and wounded here,
   We could not fly to Thee.
The friends, who in our sunshine live,
   When winter comes, are flown:
And he, who has but tears to give,
   Must weep those tears alone.
But Thou wilt heal that broken heart,
   Which, like the plans that throw
Their fragrance from the wounded part,
   Breathes sweetness out of woe.

When joy no longer soothes or cheers,
   And e'en the hope that threw
A moment's sparkle o'er our tears,
   Is dimmed and vanished too!
Oh! who would bear life's stormy doom,
   Did not Thy wing of love
Come, brightly wafting through the gloom
   Our peace-branch from above?
Then sorrow, touched by Thee, grows bright
   With more than rapture's ray;
As darkness shows us worlds of light
   We never saw by day!

Thomas Moore

Generosity is giving what you could use yourself.

Anonymous

Call unto me, and I will answer thee, and show thee great and mighty things, which thou knowest not.

Jeremiah 33 :3

I sought my soul
But my soul I could not see,
I sought my God,
But my God eluded me.
I sought my brother,
And I found all three.

Anonymous

The day, with the work God gave me to do, is done, and now He has given me the night, quiet and soothing, for rest. I will, therefore, trust myself — body and spirit — into His loving, tender care, through the mystery of sleep. As flood tides from the ocean fill each bay or inlet, so power and love and peace can fill my life to overflowing as I rest quietly, serenely, patiently, bravely, lovingly, with confidence and perfect faith.

Author unknown

Why should I feel discouraged, Why should
    the shadows come,
Why should my heart be lonely And long for
    Heav'n and home,
When Jesus is my portion? My constant Friend
    is He:
His eye is on the sparrow, And I know He
    watches me.

"Let not your heart be troubled," His tender
    word I hear,

And resting on His goodness, I lose my doubts
   and fear;
Tho' by the path He leadeth But one step I
   may see:
His eye is on the sparrow, and I know He
   watches me.

Whenever I am tempted, Whenever clouds arise,
When songs give place to sighing, When hope
   within me dies,
I draw the closer to Him, From care He sets me free;
His eye is on the sparrow, and I know He
   cares for me.

Civilla D. Martin (hymn)

God still makes house calls. All you need to do is to answer
the door.

Anonymous

You will find, as you look back upon your life, that the
moments that stand out are the moments when you have done
things for others.

Henry Drummond

Solitary confinement lasted four months. It wasn't only the
isolation that was so hard, but the constant threat that at any
moment of the day or night they would come for me.
Whenever I heard footsteps outside my cell I would ask myself, "Are they coming to torture or kill me?"
I cried out, "Lord, I'm not strong enough to endure this. I

don't have the faith!'' Suddenly I noticed an ant which I had watched roaming the floor of the cell for days. I had just mopped the floor with a wet rag, and the moment the ant felt the water on the stones, he ran straight to his tiny hole in the wall.

Then it was as if the Lord said to me, ''What about that ant? He didn't stop to look at the wet rag or his weak feet—he went straight to his hiding place. Corrie, don't look at your faith; it is weak, like the tiny feet of that ant. . . . I am your hiding place, and you can come running to Me just like that ant disappeared into that hole in the wall.''

That brought real peace into my heart. I was then fifty-three years old, and I had always known about Jesus, but there in solitary confinement I began to really understand and experience for myself that His light is stronger than the deepest darkness.

Corrie ten Boom

No one is so utterly desolate, but some heart, though unknown, responds unto his own.

Henry Wadsworth Longfellow

Who shall separate us from the love of Christ? Shall tribulation, or distress, or persecution, or famine, or nakedness, or peril, or sword? . . . Nay, in all these things we are more than conquerors through him that loved us. For I am persuaded, that neither death, nor life, nor angels, nor principalities, nor powers, nor things present, nor things to come, nor height, nor depth, nor any other creature, shall be able to separate us from the love of God, which is in Christ Jesus our Lord.

Romans 8 : 35, 37-39

Thousands have found Christ to be the answer for their loneliness. The Hebrew children were not alone when they were hurled into the fiery furnace of persecution. There was One with them like unto the Son of God. Moses wasn't alone in the Midian Desert when God came to comfort him and call him to a wider ministry. Elijah wasn't alone at the cave when God came near and spoke with the still, small voice. Paul and Silas were not alone in the Philippian jail when God came down and gave them a song at midnight. Whoever you are, Christ can give you comfort and companionship.

Billy Graham

No, I will not abandon you or leave you as orphans in the storm—I will come to you. In just a little while I will be gone from the world, but I will still be present with you.

John 14:18-19 (Living Bible)

THE HUMANITY OF JESUS

May our prayer, O Christ, awaken all Thy human reminiscences, that we may feel in our hearts the sympathizing Jesus.
    Thou hast walked this earthly vale and hast not forgotten what it is to be tired, what it is to know aching muscles, as Thou didst work long hours at the carpenter's bench.
    Thou hast not forgotten what it is to feel the sharp stabs of pain, or hunger, or thirst.
    Thou knowest what it is to be forgotten, to be lonely.
    Thou dost remember the feel of hot and scalding tears running down Thy cheeks.
O we thank Thee that Thou were willing to come to earth and share with us the weakness of the flesh, for now we know that Thou dost understand all that we are ever called upon to bear.
We know that Thou, our God, art still able to do more than

we ask or expect. So bless us, each one, not according to our deserving, but according to the riches in glory of Christ Jesus, our Lord. Amen.

Peter Marshall

Behold, I stand at the door, and knock: if any man hear My voice, and open the door, I will come in to him, and will sup with him, and he with Me.

Revelation 3:20

O the deep, deep love of Jesus,
Vast, unmeasured, boundless, free!
Rolling as a mighty ocean
In its fullness over me!
Underneath me, all around me,
Is the current of Thy love—
Leading onward, leaning homeward,
To Thy glorious rest above!

O the deep, deep love of Jesus—
Spread His praise from shore to shore!
How He loveth, ever loveth,
Changeth never, nevermore!
How He watches o'er His loved ones,
Died to call them all His own;
How for them He intercedeth,
Watcheth o'er them from the throne!

Samuel Trevor Francis (hymn)

It is the Lord who goes before you: he will be with you.

Deuteronomy 31 : 8 (RSV)

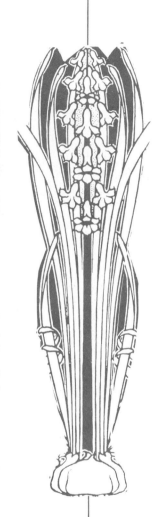

Just as there comes a warm sunbeam into every cottage window, so comes a love-beam of God's care and pity for every separate need.

Nathaniel Hawthorne

I was never less alone than when by myself.

Edward Gibbon

Who never walks save where he sees
Men's tracks, makes no discoveries.

J. G. Holland

Jesus said,"But the time is coming—in fact, it is here—when you will be scattered, each one returning to his own home, leaving me alone. Yet I will not be alone, for the Father is with me."

John 16 :32

Speak to Him, thou, for He hears,
    and Spirit with Spirit can meet—
Close is He than breathing,
    and nearer than hands and feet.

Alfred, Lord Tennyson

Norman Vincent Peale has told the story of an aging minister who lost his wife of many years. Upon hearing the news, a friend of the bereaved man went to him and persuaded the preacher to go with him to his lake cottage nearby. After a simple meal and a little conversation around a roaring log fire,

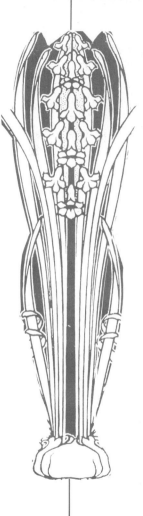

the friend put the minister to bed, tucking him in with the care a mother would give to a sick child.

"Aren't you going to bed?" the minister asked.

"No," said the friend. "I think I'll sit by the fire for a spell."

Several times through the night, the broken-hearted pastor awoke. Each time, he saw his friend sitting across the room, silhouetted by the fire he'd kept burning. It was his friend's reassuring vigil, the minister recalled later, that helped sustain him through that long, painful night. "I'd always wondered what Christ looked like. That night it came to me that He must be just like my friend who sat up all night by that open fire."

Oh, God, we go through life so lonely, needing what other people can give us, yet ashamed to show that need.

And other people go through life so lonely, hungering for what it would be such a joy for us to give.

Dear God, please bring us together, the people who need each other, who can help each other, and would so enjoy each other.

Marjorie Holmes

A man of meditation is happy, not for an hour or a day, but quite round the circle of all his years.

Isaac Taylor

Silence is the element in which great things fashion themselves.

Thomas Carlyle

9.

When You Meet with God in Prayer

When we come to God in prayer, it is important that we do so in a spirit of expectancy, because our heavenly Father has important words for us. He has encouragement for the defeated, guidance for the lost, forgiveness for the faltering, friendship for the friendless, hope for the hopeless and unconditional love for those who feel they are no longer worthy of anyone's love.

In his classic Prayer; The Mightiest Force in the World, *Frank C. Laubach advises Christians to pray with pencil and paper at hand. "When God sends a thought, write it down and keep it visible until it can be carried into action. Pray for individuals by name. Vital prayers always suggest things to be done. Indeed, prayer and action must be mates, or both are weak. The mightiest men and women on earth are strong in prayer and strong in deeds. This is the only unbeatable combination."*

He prayeth best, who loveth best
All things both great and small;
For the dear God who loveth us,
He made and loveth all.

Samuel T. Coleridge

O God, early in the morning do I cry unto Thee.
Help me to pray and to think only of Thee.
I cannot pray alone.
In me there is darkness, but with Thee there is light.

Dietrich Bonhoeffer

Your Father knoweth what things ye have need of, before ye ask him.

Matthew 6 :8

After this manner therefore pray ye: Our Father which art in heaven, Hallowed by thy name.

Thy kingdom come. Thy will be done in earth, as it is in heaven.

Give us this day our daily bread.

And forgive us our debts, as we forgive our debtors.

And lead us not into temptation, but deliver us from evil: For thine is the kingdom, and the power, and the glory, for ever. Amen.

Matthew 6 : 9-13

The time of business does not with me differ from the time of prayer; and in the noise and clatter of my kitchen, while several persons are at the same time calling for different things, I possess God in as great tranquility as if I were upon my knees at the blessed sacrament.

Brother Lawrence

Thank You, God, for little things
    that often come our way—
The things we take for granted
    but don't mention when we pray—
The unexpected courtesy,
    the thoughtful, kindly deed—
A hand reached out to help us
    in the time of sudden need—
Oh, make us more aware, dear God,
    of little daily graces
That come to us with "sweet surprise"
    from never-dreamed-of places.

Helen Steiner Rice

149

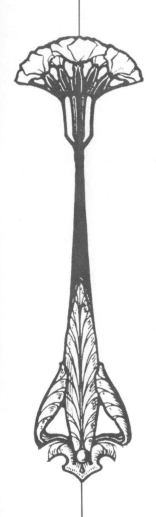

And all things, whatsoever ye shall ask in prayer, believing, ye shall receive.

Matthew 21 :22

What a friend we have in Jesus,
All our sins and griefs to bear!
What a privilege to carry
Everything to God in prayer!
O what peace we often forfeit,
O what needless pain we bear,
All because we do not carry
Everything to God in prayer.

Have we trials and temptations?
Is there trouble anywhere?
We should never be discouraged—
Take it to the Lord in prayer!
Can we find a friend so faithful,
Who will all our sorrows share?
Jesus knows our every weakness—
Take it to the Lord in prayer!

Are we weak and heavy-laden,
Cumbered with a load of care?
Precious Savior, still our refuge—
Take it to the Lord in prayer!
Do thy friends despise, forsake thee?
Take it to the Lord in prayer!
In His arms He'll take and shield thee—
Thou wilt find a solace there.

Joseph M. Scriven (hymn)

"Speak, Lord; for thy servant heareth."

I Samuel 3 :9

The prayer preceding all prayers is, 'May it be the real I who speaks. May it be the real Thou that I speak to.'

C. S. Lewis

A prayer in its simplest definition is merely a wish turned God-ward.

Phillips Brooks

Whether it's going to be a quick three-word prayer or a long heart-to-heart talk with the Lord, I first take a deep breath, feel His spirit fill me and then continue with joyful expectancy.

A. Prentice

In prayer it is better to have a heart without words, than words without a heart.

John Bunyan

Students often ask, "How do you maintain your spiritual high? What do you do on a day-to-day basis?" I tell them about my "quiet time." Some days it is in the early—sometimes late —morning, sometimes evening. Without it, my Christian life would be a wilderness. Isaiah said, "They that wait upon the Lord shall renew their strength; they shall mount up with wings as eagles, they shall run, and not be weary; and they shall walk, and not faint" (Isaiah 40:31). So gain the strength of eagles, as the prophet suggested. Set a time each day when you can spend a few minutes alone with God.

Billy Graham

I come to the garden alone,
While the dew is still on the roses;
And the voice I hear falling on my ear,
The Son of God discloses.

And He walks with me, and He talks with me,
And He tells me I am His own;
And the joy we share as we tarry there,
None other has ever known.

C. Austin Miles (hymn)

Prayer is not a vain attempt to change God's will; it is a desire to learn God's will and to share it.

George Buttrick

They never sought in vain that sought the Lord aright!

Robert Burns

More things are wrought by prayer
Than this world dreams of. Wherefore, let thy
voice
Rise like a fountain for me night and day.
For what are men better than sheep or goats
That nourish a blind life within the brain,
If, knowing God, they lift not hands of prayer
Both for themselves and those who call them
friend?
For so the whole round earth is every way
Bound by gold chains about the feet of God.

Alfred, Lord Tennyson

Saviour, I've no one else to tell
And so I trouble Thee,
I am the one forgot Thee so.
Dost Thou remember me?

Emily Dickinson

A man in one of our convenant groups lost his job unexpectedly, when his company went out of business; he came to our meeting almost in tears. He was frightened, bewildered, and desperately insecure. When he told the rest of us what had happened and was able to put words around his fears, he began to recover control of himself because he knew that he was not alone. By the next day we would begin helping him look for a new job, we would lend him money to put him through the transition period, and we would give him the moral support he would need to begin over again. But at that moment, while he was still in great pain, there was nothing any of us could do for him — except pray. Our own resources were not enough.

"Do you mind if we pray for you?" one person asked.

"No, please," our friend said.

We had no formal way of praying in such a situation. Each member prayed in words that were comfortable for him. Some used few words, others only a word, some prayed eloquently; the variety didn't matter. As the prayers began we naturally moved toward him because we felt close to him; each of us had felt as he was feeling at some time in our lives. Three or four of the men reached out and touched him on the shoulder or hand; there was great feeling of empathy. Although our situations differed, we were bound by our common need in a beauty of shared relationship.

Gradually the words came; we prayed for peace, for courage, for strength, for patience, and for healing of the hurt. Gradually our brother's shoulders began to relax, his tightly inter-

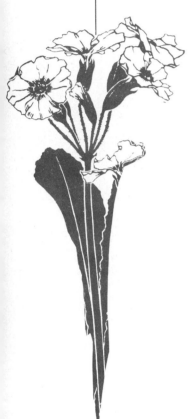

laced hands unwound, and he quietly found his brothers' arms. As the prayers ceased, he slipped down in his chair to an almost horizontal position, and his tear-filled eyes caught the gaze of each man. Then came a great theological utterance: "Wow!" He stood, raised both fists in the air, and exclaimed, "That's somethin' else!" A few embraces and bear hugs later we took our seats and a kind of silence reigned as we all savored the experience we had just had.

As the weeks wore into months, there were several more times of prayer for our brother with the laying on of hands and the prayers for perseverance. He made it and claims it was the prayers of the brothers that got him through.

Louis H. Evans, Jr.

Lord, when my soul is weary
and my heart is tired and sore,
and I have that failing feeling
that I can't take it any more;
then let me know the freshening
found in simple, childlike prayer,
when the kneeling soul knows surely
that a listening Lord is there.

Ruth Bell Graham

Ask, and it shall be given you: seek, and ye shall find; knock and it shall be opened unto you.

Matthew 7:7

Prayer is the soul's sincere desire,
Uttered or unexpressed;
The motion of a hidden fire
that trembles in the breast.

James Montgomery

It is to you personally that God speaks at this moment, and it is *through you* that He speaks when He inspires you to do some service. Be brave enough to listen at first hand to what God says to you.

John W. Harvey and Christina Yates

Thomas Beecher, brother of preacher Henry Ward Beecher, was once invited to be a substitute speaker for his famous relative. Of course, the people who had come to hear Henry—many from long distances away — were disappointed when they learned of the change. So, during the singing of the first hymn, several people in the congregation edged toward the nearest exit. Thomas motioned the pianist to stop. "Those who came to worship my brother," he announced, "may leave now. Those who came to worship God are invited to join me in the singing of the rest of the hymn."

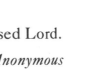

> Open our eyes, dear Lord,
> That we may see
> The far vast reaches of eternity,
> Help us to look beyond life's little cares
> So prone to fret us
> And the grief that wears
> Our courage thin.
> O may we tune our hearts
> To Thy great harmony
> That all the parts may ever be
> In perfect, sweet accord.
> Give us Thine own clear vision, blessed Lord.
>
> *Anonymous*

A mother saw her little boy sitting in a corner of the room, saying, "ABCDEFG."

"What are you doing?" she asked.

"Mom, you told me I should pray, but I have never prayed in my life and I don't know how. So I gave God the whole alphabet and asked Him to make a good prayer out of it."

That boy understood a bit of what Paul says in Romans 8:26 —that the Holy Spirit Himself helps us to pray. Yes, He prays in us.

Corrie ten Boom

How many people who pray for the Lord's help for others are willing to be one of the means by which He answers their prayers?

Anonymous

In everything by prayer and supplication with thanksgiving let your requests be made known unto God.

Philippians 4:6

I know not by what methods rare,
But this I know, God answers prayer.

Eliza M. Hickok

I have been driven many times to my knees by the overwhelming conviction that I had nowhere else to go. My own wisdom, and that of all about me, seemed insufficient for the day.

Abraham Lincoln

I asked God for strength,
  that I might achieve—
I was made weak,
  that I might learn humbly to obey.

I asked for help
  that I might do greater things—
I was given infirmity,
  that I might do better things.

I asked for riches,
  that I might be happy—
I was given poverty,
  that I might be wise.

I asked for all things,
  that I might enjoy life—
I was given life,
  that I might enjoy all things.

I got nothing
  that I asked for—
But everything
  I had hoped for.

Despite myself,
  my prayers were answered.
I am, among all men,
  most richly blessed.

An anonymous soldier of the Confederacy

God has a plan for your life — of that you can be sure.
However, God gave to each person power of choice and freedom of will. We remember how our Lord prayed, "...
nevertheless not my will, but Thine be done" (Luke 22:42).
That prayer teaches two very important truths: first, one might

have a will for his own life that is contrary to God's will for him. Second, it is possible to follow your own will and turn your back on God's will for you. Were those two facts not true, then Christ's prayer would have been mockery.

Charles L. Allen

And Satan trembles when he sees
The weakest saint upon his knees.

William Cowper

Oft have I seen at some cathedral door
   A laborer, pausing in the dust and heat,
   Lay down his burden, and with reverent feet
Enter, and cross himself, and on the floor
Kneel to repeat his paternoster o'er;
   Far off the noises of the world retreat;
   The loud vociferations of the street
Become an undistinguishable roar.

So, as I enter here from day to day,
   And leave my burden at this minster gate,
Kneeling in prayer, and not ashamed to pray,
   The tumult of the time disconsolate
To inarticulate murmurs dies away,
   While the eternal ages watch and wait.

Henry Wadsworth Longfellow

God is perfect love and perfect wisdom. We do not pray in order to change His Will, but to bring our wills into harmony with His.

William Temple

The Lord is a strong fortress. The godly run to him and are safe.

Proverbs 18 :10 (Living Bible)

PROOF

If radio's slim fingers
Can pluck a melody
From night, and toss is over
A continent or sea;

If the petaled white notes
Of a violin
Are blown across a mountain
Or a city's din;

If songs, like crimson roses,
Are culled from this blue air—
Why should mortals wonder
If God hears prayer?

Ethel Romig Fuller

He who runs from God in the morning will scarcely find Him the rest of the day.

John Bunyan

Speak, Lord, in the stillness,
While I wait on Thee;
Hushed my heart to listen
In expectancy.

Speak, O blessed Master,
In this quiet hour,

Let me see Thy face, Lord,
Feel Thy touch of power.

For the words Thou speakest,
"They are life" indeed;
Living Bread from heaven,
Now my spirit feed!

All to Thee is yielded,
I am not my own,
Blissful, glad surrender,
I am Thine alone.

Fill me with the knowledge
Of Thy glorious will;
All Thine own good pleasure
In my life fulfill.

E. May Grimes (hymn)

My words fly up; my thoughts remain below;
Words without thoughts never to heaven go.

William Shakespeare

Praying is dangerous business. Results do come.

G. Christie Swain

I DIDN'T HAVE TIME

I got up early one morning
   And rushed right into day;
I had so much to accomplish
   That I didn't have time to pray.

Problems just tumbled about me
   And heavier came each task;
"Why doesn't God help me?" I wondered.
   He answered, "You didn't ask."
I wanted to see joy and beauty
   But the day toiled on, gray and bleak.
I wondered why God didn't show me;
   He said, "But you didn't seek."
I tried to come into God's presence;
   I used all my keys at the lock.
God gently and lovingly chided,
   "My child, you didn't knock."
I woke up early this morning
   And paused before entering the day.
I had so much to accomplish
   That I had to take time to pray.

Author unknown

Remember, all God wants you to be is a little copper wire hooked up to His great power plant. He will let His will, His power, flow through you. But the only way you can get connected to the power plant of God the Father is through Jesus Christ, His Son. Then the power of the Holy Spirit will work through you.

Henrietta Mears

Pray without ceasing.

I Thessalonians 5:17

Prayer is not conquering God's reluctance, but taking hold of God's willingness.

Phillips Brooks

Who rises from prayer a better man, his prayer is answered.

George Meredith

There is nothing that makes us love a man so much as praying for him.

William Law

What does it mean when we ask for forgiveness in the Lord's Prayer? We *are* responsible for ourselves, our decisions and our actions. There is a ripple effect that spreads out from the things that we do, but there's no going back to the garden of Eden. We know the difference between good and evil and, therefore, we have the responsibility to make the best possible decisions about how we live our lives.

We know what sin is. Sin is debt—our unfulfilled obligations to one another and to God. Sin is lust—the desire to possess another for our own wishes, to possess things, to possess power beyond our need. Sin is refusing to extend our limits, the refusal to take risks, in Dietrich Bonhoeffer's great phrase, a refusal "to share the suffering of God in the life of the world." We know what sin is, and we know we need forgiveness. This petition is in the Lord's Prayer because Jesus knows we need forgiveness as much as we need our daily bread.

Maxwell G. Tow

The Lord's Prayer is not, as some fancy, the easiest, the most natural of all devout utterances. It may be committed to memory quickly, but it is slowly learned by heart.

Maurice

10.

When You Are Discouraged or Defeated

Mother had the habit of leaving little notes— poems, quotations, essays— around the house for her children to read. Her communiques to me were always left on the piano or on my violin case. One Sunday morning, she placed on the piano a little poem by Rhea F. Miller. Mother thought its message beautiful and I did, too. Instead of practicing the hymn I had intended to play that Sunday in church, I turned to this poem. Melody just seemed to form around the words.

When I had played and sung it through for the first time, Mother came from the kitchen where she had overheard. She wrapped both arms around my shoulders and placed her wet cheek next to mine. In church that morning I sang for the first time ...

> *I'd rather have Jesus than silver or gold,*
> *I'd rather be His than have riches untold,*
> *I'd rather have Jesus than houses or lands,*
> *I'd rather be led by His nail-pierced hands*
> *Than to be the king of a vast domain,*
> *Or be held in sin's dread sway,*
> *I'd rather have Jesus than anything this world affords today.*

George Beverly Shea

Be ye strong therefore, and let not your hands be weak: for your work shall be rewarded.

II Chronicles 15:7

I once thought that my handicap had robbed me forever of a full life, but then I discovered that I had everything I needed to serve God. There is only one handicap in life I have learned. That is living without the knowledge of Jesus Christ. With Him, we have everything we need.

Joni Eareckson

I have a great need for Christ;
I have a great Christ for my need.

Charles H. Spurgeon

I serve a risen Savior, He's in the world today;
I know that He is living, whatever men may say;
I see His hand of mercy, I hear His voice of cheer,
And just the time I need Him He's always near.

He lives, He lives, Christ Jesus lives today!
He walks with me and talks with me along life's narrow way.
He lives, He lives, salvation to impart!
You ask me how I know He lives? He lives within my heart.

In all the world around me I see His loving care,
And though my heart grows weary I never will despair;
I know that He is leading through all the stormy blast,
The day of His appearing will come at last.

Alfred H. Ackley   (hymn)

Faith has neither
Wall nor roof,
No concrete offering
Of proof.

Its substance frail
As winds that pass,
As image seen
In mirrored glass.

Yet mountains move
And valley fill
When faith is linked
To wish and will.

Katherine Edelman

IT COULDN'T BE DONE

Somebody said that it couldn't be done,
    But he with a chuckle replied
That "maybe it couldn't," but he would be one
    Who wouldn't say so till he'd tried.
So he buckled right in with a trace of a grin
    On his face. If he worried he hid it.
He started to sing as he tackled the thing
    That couldn't be done—and he did it!

Somebody scoffed, "Oh, you'll never do that—
    At least no one ever has done it;"
But he took off his coat and he took off his hat,
    And the first thing we knew he'd begun it.
With the lift of his chin and a bit of a grin,
    Without doubting or quiddit,
He started to sing as he tackled the thing,
    That couldn't be done—and he did it!

There are thousands to tell you it cannot be done,
    There are thousands to prophesy failure;
There are thousands to point out to you, one by one,
    The dangers that wait will assail you.
But just buckle in with a bit of a grin,
    Then take off your coat and go to it;
Just start in to sing as you tackle the thing
    That "cannot be done"—and you'll do it!

Edgar A. Guest

An admirer of Marian Anderson, the famous and beloved opera singer, remarked upon meeting her, "I'd give my right arm if I could sing like you!"

Miss Anderson smiled and replied thoughtfully, "Would you give eight hours of practice a day?"

If you are near the end of your rope, tie a knot and hang on.

Anonymous

"Is life worth living?" To scores of people, life has ceased to be worth living. To all of you, I have good news. God did not create you to be a defeated, discouraged, frustrated, wandering soul, seeking in vain for peace of heart and peace of mind. He has bigger plans for you. He has a larger orb and a greater life for you. The answer to your problem, however great, is as near as your Bible, as simple as first-grade arithmetic, and as real as your heartbeat. Upon the authority of God's Word, I tell you that Christ is the answer to every baffling perplexity wich plagues mankind. In Him is found the cure for care, a balm for bereavement, a healing for our hurts, and a sufficiency for our insufficiency.

Billy Graham

God hath not promised
Skies always blue,
Flower-strewn pathways
All our lives through;
God hath not promised
Sun without rain,
Joy without sorrow,
Peace without pain.

But God hath promised
Strength for the day,
Rest for the labor,
Light for the way,
Grace for the trials,
Help from above,
Unfailing sympathy,
Undying love.

Annie Johnson Flint

Count it all joy...when you meet various trials, for you know that the testing of your faith produces steadfastness.

James 1:2

SOMETHING GOOD IS GOING TO HAPPEN TO YOU.

Sometimes we act as if we think God is not willing to give, not ready to help us, and by our attitude of doubt and negative anticipation, we rob ourselves of God's gifts. Our miracle can only begin when we cease being negative and start being positive, when we recognize part of the problem is inside us. Regardless of how much power God has, miracle power will never fully be effective in our lives until we cooperate, until we fully expect something good to happen.

Oral Roberts

Only believe, only believe,
All things are possible,
Only believe.

Paul Radar   (hymn)

The story is told of a woman who complained to God about the weight of her cross. "It is simply too much for me to bear," she cried. The Lord was sympathetic. "Give me your cross," He said, "and I'll put it in a sack with all the other crosses people have to bear. Then you can choose another one." She readily agreed, but each cross she drew from the bag was too heavy. Finally, near the bottom, she found one much lighter than the rest. "I'll take this one, Lord," she said, satisfied at last. "Fine," He answered, "but you should know that that's the very cross you had before."

Got any rivers you think are uncrossable?
Got any mountains you can't tunnel through?
God specializes in things thought impossible;
He does what others cannot do.

Oscar Eliason   (hymn)

With men this is impossible; but with God all things are possible.

Matthew 19:26

Contentment is not satisfaction. It is the grateful, faithful, fruitful use of what we have, little or much. It is to take the cup of Providence, and call upon the name of the Lord. What the cup contains is its contents. To get all there is in the cup is the act and art of contentment. Not to drink because one has but half a cup, or because one does not like its flavor, or because someone else has silver to one's own glass, is to lose the contents; and that is the penalty, if not the meaning of discontent. No one is discontented who employs and enjoys to the utmost what he has. It is high philosophy to say, we can have just what we like if we like what we have; but this much at least can be done (and this is contentment): to have the most and best in life, by making the most and best of what we have.

Maltbie D. Babcock

God has a thousand ways
Where I can see not one;
When all my means have reached their end
Then His have just begun.

Esther Guyot

I have an old friend, an excellent person, whose witness once helped me to see that the seeking of God's guidance is, despite all our mistakes, the surest rule of life. Caught up in the tragic events of the war, he found himself facing a serious decision. He prayed, he meditated with some friends. He made the choice that seemed to him to conform with God's will. But the course of events made him doubt whether he had made the right decision. He underwent an inner crisis. He came to spend a few days with me. Every morning we read the Bible together, before our meditation. On the last day we had read the story of Lot's wife, who was turned into a pillar of salt because she looked back (Genesis 19:26). Then my friend exclaimed, "I am like Lot's wife. My life is petrified because I keep looking back. I turn that old problem over and over in my mind, uselessly, without ever discovering whether I did right or not. My life is no longer an adventure, because my faith is shaken and I am not looking for God's guidance any more. I want to start going forward again." Shortly afterward a message from a friend who had died for his country finally relit in him the flame of dedication to Christ, and his life once more bore fruit.

Paul Tournier

Do what you can, with what you have, where you are.

Theodore Roosevelt

For in order to mount to the Cross, the summit of sacrifice, ... Christ passed through all the stages which the man who struggles passes through. All—and that is why His suffering is so familiar to us; that is why we pity Him, and why His final victory seems to us so much our own future victory.

That part of Christ's nature which was profoundly human helps us to understand Him and love Him. ... If He had not

within Him this warm human element, He would never be able to touch our hearts with such assurance and tenderness; He would not be able to become a model for our lives. We struggle, we see Him struggle also, and we find strength. We see that we are not all alone in the world; He is fighting at our side.

Nikos Kazantzakis

Jesus now has many lovers of His heavenly Kingdom, but few bearers of His cross.

Thomas à Kempis

A mighty fortress is our God,
A bulwark never failing;
Our helper He amid the flood
Of mortal ills prevailing.
For still our ancient foe
Doth seek to work us woe—
His craft and power are great,
And, armed with cruel hate,
On earth is not His equal.

Did we in our own strength confide,
Our striving would be losing,
Were not the right man on our side,
The man of God's own choosing.
Dost ask who that may be?
Christ Jesus, it is He—
Lord Sabaoth His name,
From age to age the same,
And He must win the battle.

Martin Luther (hymn)

For if you had faith even as small as a tiny mustard seed you could say to this mountain, 'Move!' and it would go far away. Nothing would be impossible.

Matthew 17:20 (Living Bible)

When poet John Masefield was still a struggling writer he began to doubt that he had the ability to succeed in his chosen profession. One day he came upon a simple verse, and he credited these lines with helping sustain him through his days of discouragement:

> Sitting still and wishing
> Makes no person great.
> The good Lord sends the fishing,
> But you must dig the bait.

But they that wait upon the Lord shall renew their strength; they shall mount up with wings as eagles; they shall run, and not be weary; and they shall walk, and not faint.

Isaiah 40:31

When Jean Francois Millet, the painter of the "Angelus," worked on his almost divine canvas in which the very air seems pulsing with the regenerating esssence of spiritual reverence, he was painting against time, he was antidoting sorrow, he was racing against death. His brush strokes, put on in the early morning hours before he went to his menial duties as a railway porter, ... meant strength, food and medicine for the dying wife he adored. The art failure that cast time into the depths of poverty unified with marvelous intensity all the finer elements of his nature. This rare spiritual unity, this purging of all the dross of triviality as he passed through the furnace of poverty, trial and sorrow gave eloquence to his brush and enabled him to paint as never before, as no prosperity would have made possible.

William George Jordan

Oh, Jesus is a Rock in a weary land,
A shelter in the time of storm.

Ira D. Sankey   (hymn)

Anxious hearts are very heavy but a word of encouragement does wonders!

Proverbs 12 :25 (Living Bible)

Life is a mixture
   of sunshine and rain,
Laughter and teardrops,
   Pleasure and pain—
Low tides and high tides,
   Mountains and plains,
Triumphs, defeats,
   and losses and gains—
But there never was a cloud
That the SUN didn't SHINE THROUGH
And there's nothing that's IMPOSSIBLE
For Jesus Christ to do!

Helen Steiner Rice

It's good to have money and the things that money can buy, but it's good, too, to check up once in a while and make sure you haven't lost the things that money can't buy.

George Horace Lorimer

175

A small boy working in a Naples, Italy, factory aspired to be a singer but at the age of ten he was told by a voice teacher, "You can't sing. Your voice sounds like wind in the shutters."

His mother scoffed at the teacher. She knew that her son loved to sing more than anything else in the world, and she encouraged him to continue. She also prayed for him daily, and made numerous sacrifices, even going without shoes, to pay for his lessons. Her faith was more than rewarded. Not many years later the world of music owed a huge debt to the mother of Enrico Caruso.

Consider
The lilies of the field, whose bloom is brief—
We are as they;
Like them we fade away,
As doth a leaf.

Consider
The sparrows of the air, of small account:
Our God doth view
Whether they fall or mount—
He guards us too.

Consider
The lilies, that do neither spin nor toil,
Yet are most fair—
What profits all his care,
And all this coil?

Consider
The birds, that have no barn nor harvest-weeks:
God gives them food—
Much more our Father seeks
To do us good.

Christina Rossetti

Men fail much oftener from want of perseverance than from want of talent.

William Cobbett

Sometimes life has a way of putting us on our backs in order to force us to look up.

Charles L. Allen

The King of love my shepherd is,
Whose goodness faileth never;
I nothing lack if I am his,
And he is mine forever.

Henry W. Baker (hymn)

O Lord God, when Thou givest to Thy servants to endeavor any great matter, grant us also to know that it is not the beginning but the continuing of the same until it be thoroughly finished which yieldeth the true glory.

Sir Francis Drake

Conditions in our barracks in the concentration camp at Ravensbruck were terrible. When we first arrived I told Betsie I could not bear the lice that lived in our filthy blankets and mattresses. She replied, "You must thank God for everything, even for lice." Betsie was right. Because of the bugs which infested our barracks, the women guards and officers kept their distance, and we were able to hold our Bible studies without fear. God had a use for the vermin, after all! How much more simple it would be if we would learn to thank God for everything instead of using our own judgment.

Corrie ten Boom

God whispers to us in our pleasures, speaks to us in our conscience, but shouts in our pain; it is his megaphone to rouse a deaf world.

C. S. Lewis

When we are defeated, let us remember that it is part of the business of living at its highest. If you never take a chance you will never be defeated — but you will never accomplish anything either. Also, if you never know defeat it means that you were never willing to take a chance, and that should make us more devastated than the fact that we were defeated. Jesus said, "He that findeth his life shall lose it." If you are defeated in life, most of the time it means that you took a chance. If you are afraid to take a chance and only concerned with saving your life and never tasting defeat, it is a certainty that eventually your defeat will be total and permanent. It is just as much a sin to be too careful as it is to take too many chances.

Charles L. Allen

Who would true valour see,
Let him come hither;
One here will constant be,
Come wind, come weather;
There's no discouragement
Shall make him once relent
His first avowed intent
To be a pilgrim.

John Bunyan

I awoke in the dark with one thought that blazed for a moment. The only treasure I can take with me when I leave this life is my knowledge of Christ. In times of pain, I draw closer to Him. Therefore, I am richer in trouble.

Laurel Lee

11.

When You Yearn for Serenity and Peace

How can one find peace in the midst of turmoil? Calm in the face of adversity and defeat? Nothing sustains people who have suffered tribulations like an indomitable faith in Jesus Christ.

Businessman H. G. Spafford lost everything he owned in the famous Chicago fire of 1871, but it did not compare with the loss he was to suffer a short time later when the ship upon which his wife and four childen were sailing sank enroute to

Europe. His wife was rescued but the children were lost. Mr. Spafford immediately set sail on another ship to join her. Several nights later the captain pointed out the spot where the other ship had gone down.

Filled with grief, Mr. Spafford went to his cabin where he wrote a poem that reflected his deep faith, a poem that would later be set to music and would give comfort to countless others seeking a peace that "passes understanding." The words he wrote were these:

> *When peace, like a river, attendeth my way,*
> *When sorrows like sea billows roll—*
> *Whatever my lot, Thou hast taught me to say,*
> *It is well, it is well with my soul.*

Thou wilt keep him in perfect peace, whose mind is stayed on thee: because he trusteth in thee.

Isaiah 26:3

O Thou,
Whose stillness drowns
earth's total noise—
its grating sounds:
progress,
traffic,
voice;
flutterings
of my frustration,
mutterings,

agitation;
the screaming silences
without,
within;
the din
of questions clamoring
for their "why?"
and "how?"
now!
the rumblings
of man's discontent,
erupting hate,
violence;
war's distant thunder
rolling near,
and everywhere
the cries
of fear
that paralyzes
as it grips...
and near at hand
a faucet drips.

O Thou,
Whose stillness drowns
earth's total noise,
only in Thee
is stillness found...
And I
rejoice.

Ruth Bell Graham

I know not what I shall become: it seems to me that peace
of soul and repose of spirit descend on me, even in sleep. To be
without the sense of this peace, would be affliction indeed....

I know not what God purposes with me, or keeps me for; I am in a calm so great that I fear naught. What can I fear, when I am with Him: and with Him, in His Presence, I hold myself the most I can. May all things praise Him.

Brother Lawrence

THE SEASONS OF THE SOUL

Why am I cast down
　　and despondently sad
When I long to be happy
　　and joyous and glad?
Why is my heart heavy
　　with unfathomable weight
As I try to escape
　　this soul-saddened state?
I ask myself often—
　　"What makes life this way,
Why is the song silenced
　　in the heart that was gay?"
And then with God's help
　　it all becomes clear.
The *Soul* has its *Seasons*
　　just the same as the year—
I too must pass through
　　life's autumn of dying,
A desolate period
　　of heart-hurt and crying,
Followed by winter
　　in whose frostbitten hand
My heart is as frozen
　　as the snow-covered land—
Yes, man too must pass
　　through the seasons God sends,

Content in the knowledge
   that everything ends.
And oh what a blessing
   to know there are reasons
And to find that our soul
   must, too, have its seasons—
Bounteous Seasons
   and *Barren Ones*, too,
Times for rejoicing
   and times to be blue,
But meeting these seasons
   of dark desolation
With strength that is born
   of anticipation
That comes from knowing
   That "autumn-time sadness'
Will surely be followed
   by a "Springtime of Gladness."

                              Helen Steiner Rice

Grace to you and peace from God our Father and the Lord
Jesus Christ.

                              Romans 1 :7

SLOW ME DOWN, LORD!

Slow me down, Lord!
Ease the pounding of my heart by the quieting of my mind.
   Steady my hurried pace, with a vision of the eternal reach of
time. Give me, amidst the confusion of my day, the calmness
of the everlasting hills. Break the tension of my nerves with the
soothing music of the singing streams that live in my memory.

Help me to know the magical restoring power of sleep. Teach me the art of taking minute vacations of slowing down. To look at a flower; to chat with an old friend or make a new one; to pet a stray dog; to watch a spider build a web; to smile at a child; or to read from a good book.

Remind me each day that the race is not always to the swift; that there is more to life than increasing its speed.

Inspire me to send my roots deep into the soil of life's enduring values that I may grow towards the stars of my greater destiny.

Orin L. Crane

Thanks be to Thee, my Lord Jesus Christ,
For all the benefits Thou hast given me,
For all the pains and insults Thou
   hast borne for me.
O most merciful Redeemer, Friend, and
   Brother,
May I know Thee more clearly,
May I love Thee more dearly,
May I follow Thee more nearly.

Twelfth-century prayer

To every thing there is a season,
   and a time to every purpose
   under the heaven:
A time to be born, and a time to die;
   a time to plant, and a time to
   pluck up that which is planted;
A time to kill, and a time to heal;
   a time to break down,
   and a time to build up;

184

A time to weep, and a time to laugh;
   a time to mourn, and a time to dance;
A time to cast away stones,
   and a time to gather stones together;
   a time to embrace,
   and a time to refrain from embracing;
A time to get, and a time to lose;
   a time to keep, and a time to cast away;
A time to rend, and a time to sew;
   a time to keep silence,
   and a time to speak;
A time to love, and a time to hate;
   a time of war, and a time of peace.

Ecclesiastes 3 : 1-8

Tis pleasant, through the loopholes of retreat,
To peep at such a world, to see the stir,
Of the great Babel; and not feel the crowd.

William Cowper

   Don't worry about anything; instead pray about everything; tell God your needs and don't forget to thank him for his answers. If you do this you will experience God's peace, which is far more wonderful than the human mind can understand. His peace will keep your thoughts and your hearts quiet and at rest as you trust in Christ Jesus.

Philippians 4 :6-7 (Living Bible)

185

Several years ago Mother Teresa of Calcutta, India, was introduced to an overflow congregation at Washington's National Presbyterian Church which included people from every part of Christendom. It was the first time this saintly Roman Catholic had ever spoken in a Prostestant church.

A tiny Albanian woman of God, dressed in a simple unbleached muslin habit with bands of faded blue on the edges, Mother Teresa stood simply at the front of the sanctuary and spoke briefly on the work of the Sisters of Charity among the poorest of the poor who are dying each day in the slums of Calcutta. It was in the name of these same people that she would accept the Nobel Prize for Peace in 1979.

We were all melted down by the love that shone from the depths of her eyes and spread over her care-lined, yet joyful face. I was not the only one in the congregation with tears as I listened to her softly spoken words about how blessed it is to live in poverty and to share the suffering of God's childen. And I'll never forget the perfect way she summed it up, putting to shame forever all "good works" that don't originate in the heart of God: "It is not that you serve the rich or the poor. It is the love you put into the doing."

A part of the daily prayer of Mother Teresa and her co-workers goes like this: "Make us worthy, Lord, to serve our fellowmen throughout the world who live and die in poverty and hunger. Give them through our hands their daily bread, and by our understanding give peace and joy."

Colleen Townsend Evans

Jesus calls us o'er the tumult
Of our life's wild, restless sea;
Day by day I hear Him saying,
"Christian, come and follow me."

As, of old, disciples heard it
By the Galilean lake,

Turning from home and work and leisure,
Leaving all for His dear sake,

In our joys and in our sorrows,
Days of toil and hours of ease,
Still He calls in cares and pleasures,
"Christian, love me more than these."

Jesus calls us: by Thy mercies,
Savior, may we hear Thy call,
Give our hearts to Thine obedience,
Serve and love Thee best of all.

Cecil Frances Alexander (hymn)

I am not an emotional person. I don't know why, but I don't cry very easily. But of the few times I have cried in my life, some of them have been over sin that I committed many years ago. The night I came to Christ, I didn't have any tears. But later I went home and I looked out my window at the North Carolina sky and I cried over my sins. I said, "Oh God, forgive me." And the most wonderful peace swept over my soul.

Billy Graham

When the Holy Spirit controls our lives he will produce this kind of fruit in us: love, joy, peace, patience, kindness, goodness, faithfulness, gentleness and self-control.

Galatians 5:22-23 (Living Bible)

For God is not the author of confusion but of peace.

I Corinthians 14:33

The secret of a happy and successful life is to be content with the abilities God gave and discontented with the use you make of them.

Burton Hillis

Keep us, oh God, from all smallness. Let us be large in thought, in word, and in deed. Let us have done with complaint, and leave off all self-seeking. May we put away all pretense, and meet each other with pity and without prejudice. May we never be hasty in Judgment of others. Make us always generous. Let us take time to be calm and gentle. Teach us to put into action our better impulses, and to walk unafraid. Grant that we may realize that the little things of life are those which create our differences, and that in the big things of life, we are as one under God. And, O Lord, let us never forget to be kind.

Mary, Queen of Scots

I am only one,
But still I am one.
I cannot do everything,
But still I can do something;
And because I cannot do everything
I will not refuse to do the something that I can do."

Edward Everett Hale

If it be possible, as much as lieth in you, live peaceably with all men.

Romans 12:18

The calmness bends serene above
    My restlessness to still;
Around me flows Thy quickening life,
    To nerve my faltering will;
Thy presence fills my solitude;
Thy providence turns all to good.

Henry Wadsworth Longfellow

We seek God's peace, a quiet contentment, and know that it is good. But is there a germ of truth is what Thomas Alva Edison said? "Restlessness is discontent—and discontent is the first necessity of progress. Show me a *thoroughly* satisfied man—and I will show you a failure." Prayerfully consider if your restlessness, your dissatisfaction with the *status quo*, might not be the Lord's nudging.

C. Borden

Innocent and infinite are the pleasures of observation.

Henry James

Thou hast touched me, and I have been translated into thy peace.

Saint Augustine

Joys are flowing like a river,
Since the Comforter has come;
He abides with us forever,
Makes the trusting heart His home.

    Blessed quietness, holy quietness,
    What assurance in my soul!

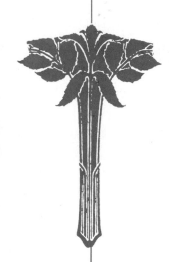

On the stormy sea He speaks peace to me,
How the billows cease to roll!

Bring life and health and gladness,
All around this heav'nly Guest,
Banished unbelief and sadness
Changed our weariness to rest.

Like the rain that falls from heaven,
Like the sunlight from the sky,
So the Holy Ghost is given,
Coming on us from on high.

Manie P. Ferguson (hymn)

There is peace in God's will because it brings to us the approval of a good conscience. I cannot explain exactly what the conscience is or how it works, but I can say that within every one of us there is a voice saying what is right and what is wrong. When we do what God wants us to do, it makes us feel good inside. Really, there is no greater happiness to be found in life than to do what Jesus did when he lifted his eyes to heaven and said, "I have finished the work which thou gavest me to do."

Charles L. Allen

Come unto me, all ye that labour
and are heavy laden,
and I will give you rest.
Take my yoke upon you, and learn of me;
for I am meek and lowly in heart:
and ye shall find rest unto your souls.
For my yoke is easy, and my burden is light.

Matthew 11:28-30

Serenity comes not alone by removing the outward causes and occasions of fear, but by the discovery of inward reservoirs to draw upon.

Rufus M. Jones

Are you weary? Rest a little bit.
In some quiet corner, fold your hands and sit.
Do not let the trials that have grieved you all the day
Haunt this quiet corner; drive them all away!
Let your heart grow empty of every thought unkind
That peace may hover round you, and joy may fill your mind.
Count up all your blessings, I'm sure they are not few,
That the dear Lord daily just bestows on you.
Soon you'll feel so rested, glad you stopped a bit,
In this quiet corner, to fold your hands and sit.

Anonymous

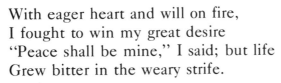

With eager heart and will on fire,
I fought to win my great desire
"Peace shall be mine," I said; but life
Grew bitter in the weary strife.

My soul was tired, and my pride
Was wounded deep: to Heaven I cried,
"God grant me peace or I must die,"
The dumb stars glittered no reply.

Broken at last, I bowed my head,
Forgetting all myself, and said,
"Whatever comes, His will be done";
And in that moment peace was won.

Henry Van Dyke

191

The Lord will give strength unto his people; the Lord will bless his people with peace."

Psalm 29 :11

And he arose, and rebuked the wind, and said unto the sea. Peace, be still. And the wind ceased and there was a great calm.

Mark 4 :39

Let there peace on earth, and let it begin with me.
Let there be peace on earth, the peace that was meant to be.
With God as our Father, brothers all are we.
Let me walk with my brother in perfect harmony.
Let peace begin with me; let this be the moment now,
With every step I take, let this be my solemn vow!
To take each moment, and live each moment in peace
    eternally!
Let there be peace on earth, and let it begin with me.

Sy Miller and Jill Jackson   (hymn)

Let your souls lie down upon the couch of His sweet will, as your bodies lie down in their beds at night. Relax every strain, and lay off every burden. Let yourself go in a perfect abandonment of ease and comfort, sure that since He holds you up, you are perfectly safe. Your part is simply to rest. His part is to sustain you; and He cannot fail . . . "Thou wilt keep him in perfect peace, whose mind is stayed on thee: because he trusteth in thee." This is the Divine description of the life of faith about which I am writing. It is no speculative theory, neither is it a dream of romance. There is such a thing as having one's soul kept in perfect peace, now and here in this life; and childlike trust in God is the key to its attainment.

Hannah Whitall Smith

Calm soul of all things, make it mine
To feel amid the city's jar
That there exists a peace of thine
Man did not make and cannot mar.

Matthew Arnold

O Great spirit!
Thou hast made this lake;
Thou hast also created us as Thy children;
Thou art able to make this water calm
Until we have safety passed over.

Chippewa Indian prayer

Peace I leave with you, my peace I give unto you: not as the world giveth, give I unto you.

John 14 :27

At the heart of the cyclone tearing the sky
And flinging the clouds and the towers by,
    Is a place of central calm;

So here in the roar of mortal things,
I have a place where my spirit sings,
   In the hollow of God's Palm.

Edwin Markham

Spirit of God, descend upon my heart;
Wean it from earth, through all its pulses move;
Stoop to my weakness, mighty as Thou art,
And make me love Thee as I ought to love.

I ask no dream, no prophet ecstasies,
No sudden rending of the veil of clay,
No angel visitant, no opening skies;
But take the dimness of my soul away.

George Croly   (hymn)

There is but one way to tranquility of mind and happiness, and that is to account no external things thine own, but to commit all to God.

Epictetus

TRUE REST

Rest is not quitting
   The busy career;
Rest is the fitting
   Of self to one's sphere.

'Tis the brook's motion,
   Clear without strife,

Fleeting to ocean,
    After this life.

'Tis loving and serving,
    The highest and best;
'This onward, unswerving,
    And this is true rest.

Johann Wolfgang von Goethe

I am a man of peace. I believe in peace. But I do not want peace at any price. I do not want peace that you find in stone; I do not want the peace you find in the grave; but I do want the peace which you find embedded in the human breast, which is exposed to the arrows of the whole world, but which is protected from all harm by the power of Almighty God.

Mahatma Gandhi

Breathe, O breathe Thy loving Spirit
Into ev'ry troubled breast;
Let us all in Thee inherit,
Let us find Thy promised rest.

Charles Wesley (hymn).

The Lord bless thee, and keep thee:
The Lord make his face shine upon thee,
    and be gracious unto thee:
The Lord lift up his countenance upon thee,
    and give thee peace.

Numbers 6:24—26

Close now thine eyes and rest secure;
Thy soul is safe enough, thy body sure;
He that loves thee, He that keeps
And guards thee, never slumbers, never sleeps.
The smiling conscience in a sleeping breast
Has only peace, has only rest;
The music and the mirth of kings
Are but very discords, when she sings.
Then close thine eyes and rest secure:
No sleep so sweet as thine, no rest so sure.

Francis Quarles

Lord, grant us peace; for all we have and are has come from you."

Isaiah 26 :12 (Living Bible)

Far away in the depth of my spirit tonight
Rolls a melody sweeter than psalm;
In celestial–like strains it unceasingly falls
O'er my soul like an infinite calm.
Peace! Peace! wonderful peace,
Coming down from the Father above;
Sweep over my spirit forever I pray,
In fathomless billows of love.

W. D. Cornell (hymm)

As we study New Testament Christianity, we are aware that there is an inner core of tranquility and stability . . . It was not mere absence of strife or conflict, [but] a positive peace, a solid foundation which held fast amid all the turmoil of human experience.

J. B. Phillips

12.

When You Need Courage and Wisdom to Face the Road Ahead

A woman who had served with Sir Wilfred Grenfell, the famous doctor and humanitarian, told of a terrible storm their hospital ship had once encountered along the rocky coast of Newfoundland. "We were ferrying patients to a base hospital, and waves threatened to capsize the ship. I hoped that we'd try to find a safe harbor, but the coast was

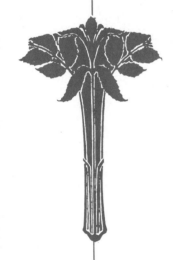

shrouded by fog and Sir Wilfred kept to his course and finally brought the ship safely to our destination."

"Were you afraid ?" he asked her afterward.

"I was too busy with the patients," she answered. "Were you ?"

"The only thing I've ever feared," Grenfell told her, "is the loss of courage and faith. If Jesus is the master of your life, there is no room for fear. When two courses are open, He asks us to take the more venturesome one if it means helping others."

Be strong and of a good courage; be not afraid, neither be thou dismayed; for the Lord thy God is with thee whithersoever thou goest.

Joshua 1 :9

Great is Thy faithfulness, O God my Father!
There is no shadow of turning with Thee;
Thou changest not, Thy compassions, they fail not:
As Thou hast been Thou forever wilt be.
Great is Thy faithfulness,
Great is Thy faithfulness,
Morning by morning new mercies I see;
All I have needed Thy hand hath provided—
Great is Thy faithfulness, Lord, unto me!

Thomas O. Chisholm   (hymn)

Do not pray for easy lives. Pray to be stronger men! Do not pray for tasks equal to your powers. Pray for powers equal to your tasks.

Phillips Brooks

God,
give us grace to accept with serenity
the things that cannot be changed,
courage to change the things
which should be changed,
and the wisdom to distinguish
the one from the other.

Reinhold Niebuhr

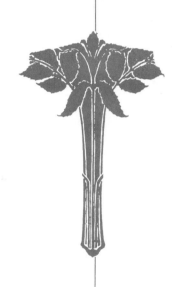

God moves in a mysterious way
His wonders to perform;
He plants His footsteps in the sea
And rides upon the storm.

You fearful saints, fresh courage take:
The clouds you so much dread
Are big with mercy, and shall break
In blessings on your head.

William Cowper (hymn)

Doing God's will involves body, mind and spirit, not just spirit alone. Bringing the body under obedience means going to bed at a sensible hour, grooming yourself carefully, watching your weight, cutting out the junk food. And it means when the alarm goes off, your feet hit the floor. You have to *move*.

Elizabeth Elliot Leitch

Wait on the Lord: be of good courage, and he shall strengthen thine heart: wait, I say, on the Lord.

Psalm 27 : 14

Earthly props are useless,
    On Thy grace I fall;
Earthly strength is weakness,
    Father, on Thee I call - -
For comfort, strength, and guidance,
    O, give me all!

John Oxenham

THE COURAGEOUS

They on the heights are not the souls
    who never erred nor went astray
Who trod unswerving toward their goals
    Along a smooth, rose-bordered way.
Nay! those who stand where first comes dawn
Are those who stumbled—but went on!

Anonymous

It is one of the most beautiful compensations of life that no man can sincerely try to help another without helping himself.

Ralph Waldo Emerson

There are two days of the week upon which and about which I never worry—two carefree days kept sacredly free from worry and apprehension. One of these days is yesterday. Yesterday with its cares and frets and all its pain and aches, all its faults, its mistakes and blunders, has passed forever beyond recall. It was mine; it is God's. And the other day that I do not worry about is tomorrow. Tomorrow with all its possible adversities, its burdens, its perils, its large promise and poor performance, its failures and mistakes, is as far beyond my mastery as its dead sister, yesterday. Tomorrow is God's day; it will be mine.

There is left for myself, then, but one day in the week—today.

Robert J. Burdette

The heights of great men reached and kept
Were not attained by sudden flight,
But they while their companions slept
Were toiling upward in the night.

Henry Wadsworth Longfellow

Be still, my soul! thy God doth undertake
To guide the future as He has the past.
Thy hope, thy confidence let nothing shake;
All now mysterious shall be bright at last.
Be still, my soul! the waves and winds still know
His voice who ruled them while He dwelt below.

Katharina von Schlegel   (hymn)

Leslie Weatherhead, the famous British minister and writer, told the World War II story of a young soldier who, despite the objections of his commanding officer, went to the aid of a dying buddy caught between the lines. Through he managed to reach his fallen friend, it was too late to save him and the brave rescuer was mortally wounded himself while returning to his platoon. "I told you not to go," the officer cried over the bleeding man. "It was not worth it." "Yes, it was, the soldier replied. "It was worth it because when I got to him he said, 'I knew you'd come.'

The way to have a better tomorrow is to start working on it today.

Anonymous

When we walk with the Lord
In the light of His Word,
What a glory He sheds on our way!
While we do His good will,
He abides with us still,
And with all who will trust and obey.

Trust and obey, for there's no other way
To be happy in Jessus, but to trust and obey.

James H. Sammis (hymn)

No act of kindness, no matter how small, is ever wasted.

Aesop

Once I could accept my own mortality—that God gives each of us just one day at a time—only then could I really begin to *live*! Now I realize that each day is precious . . . and not to be wasted.

Christina Andrews

202

If I can stop one heart from breaking,
I shall not live in vain;
If I can ease one life the aching,
Or cool one pain,
Or help one fainting robin
Unto his nest again,
I shall not live in vain.

Emily Dickinson

I can do all things through Christ which strengtheneth me.

Phillippians 4 :13

A PARENT'S PRAYER

Lord, teach me understanding
That I may know the way to my child's heart and mind;
Give me strength,
That I not fail him in minor tragedies or in great crises;
Give me courage,
That I may stand firm when he is wrong, or wayward, or
    heedless;
Grant me humility,
That I may acknowledge my own mistake when he is right.

Gordon Phillips

It's good to remember that not even the Master shepherd
can lead if the sheep do not follow Him but insist on running
ahead of Him or taking side paths.

Catherine Marshall

Missionary E. Stanley Jones told the story of an unnamed king who once had wires stretched between the towers of two castles he owned, hoping to create harp-line music when the wind blew. But he was greatly disappointed. When the winds came, only a faint sound was heard, only a few weak notes.

However, one night a mighty storm descended upon the kingdom, one that threatened life and limb. Yet it was something else that roused the king from his sleep: a heavenly music that emanated from the storm-whipped wires stretched between the two castles. In life, too, Dr. Jones pointed out, it often takes winds of great adversity to bring out the best in us.

Courage, brother! do not stumble,
Though thy path be dark as night;
There's a star to guide the humble,
Trust in God and do the right.

Norman MacLeod

You see things as they are; and you ask, "Why?" But I dream things that never were: and I ask "Why not?"

George Bernard Shaw

Be Thou my Vision, O Lord of my heart;
Nought be all else to me, save that Thou art—
Thou my best thought, by day or by night,
Waking or sleeping, Thy presence my light.

Be Thou my Wisdom, and Thou my true Word;
I ever with Thee and Thou with me, Lord;
Thou my great Father, I thy true son;
Thou in me dwelling, and I with Thee one.

Riches I heed not, nor man's empty praise,
Thou mine inheritance, now and always;
Thou and Thou only, first in my heart,
High King of heaven, my Treasure Thou art.

High King of heaven, my victory's won,
May I reach heaven's joys, O bright heaven's Sun!
Heart of my own heart, whatever befall,
Still be my Vision, O Ruler of all.

Ancient Irish hymn
(translated by Mary Byrne)

Courage is not simply one of the virtues, but the form of every virtue at the testing point, which means at the point of highest reality. A chastity or honesty or mercy which yields to danger will be chaste or honest or merciful only on conditions. Pilate was merciful till it became risky.

C. S. Lewis

A poor man served by thee shall make thee rich;
A sick man helped by thee shall make thee strong;
Thou shalt be served thyself by every sense
Of service which thou renderest.

Elizabeth Barrett Browning

We are learning to turn again and again to the Lord of present moment to find the eternal quality of life of which Christ spoke (John 17:3).

Not long ago, I heard a story which helped me see again the parodoxical power in living in the *Now*. Several years ago a very busy business executive in an eastern city was running to catch a train. He had about given up trying to live a "personal" daily

life because of the great demands on his time — speaking engagements and administrative duties in his organization. This particular morning en route to Grand Central Station he promised himself that he would try to *be* a Christian that day instead of only talking about it. By the time he had picked up his ticket, he was late. Charging across the lobby with his bags and down the ramp, he heard the last "all aboard." He was about to get on the train when he bumped into a small child with his suitcase. The little boy had been carrying a new jigsaw puzzle, the pieces of which were now scattered all over the platform.

The executive paused, saw the child in tears, and with an inward sigh, stopped, smiled and helped the boy pick up his puzzle, as the train pulled out.

The child watched him intently. When they finished picking up all of the pieces, the little boy looked at the man with a kind awe. "Mister," he said hesitantly, "are you *Jesus?*"

And for the moment the man realized that—on that platform—he had been.

Keith Miller

TEN MISTAKES TO AVOID

Remorse over yesterday's failure.
Anxiety over today's problem.
Worry over tomorrow's uncertainty.
Waist of the moment's opportunity.
Procrastination with one's present duty.
Resentment of another's success.
Criticism of a neighbor's imperfection.
Impatience with youth's immaturity.
Skepticism of our nation's future.
Unbelief in God's providence.

William Arthur Ward

Be not afraid, but speak, and hold not thy peace: For I am with thee, and no man shall set on thee to hurt thee.

Acts 18:9,10

The person who often looks up to God rarely looks down on any man.

William Arthur Ward

You shall cross the barren dessert,
But you shall not die of thirst.
You shall wander far in safety
Though you do not know the way.
You shall speak your words to foreign men
And they will understand.
You shall see the face of God and live.

    Be not afraid.
    I go before you always.
    Come follow Me,
    And I will give you rest.

If you pass through raging waters in the sea,
You shall not drown.
If you walk amid the burning flames,
You shall not be harmed.
If you stand before the pow'r of hell
And death is at your side,
Know that I am with you through it all.

Bob Dufford (hymn)

Whatever enlarges hope will also exalt courage.

Samuel Johnson

ONE SOLITARY LIFE

He was born in an obscure village. He worked in a carpenter shop until he was thirty. He then became an itinerant preacher. He never held an office. He never had a family or owned a house. He didn't go to college. He had no credentials but himself . . .

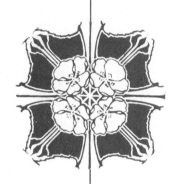

Nineteen centuries have come and gone, and today he is the central figure of the human race. All the armies that ever marched, and all the navies that ever sailed, all the parliments that ever sat, and all the kings that ever reigned have not affected the life of man on this earth as much as that . . . one solitary life.

Author unknown.

Take the name of Jesus with you,
Child of sorrow and of woe.
It will joy and comfort give you,
Take it then where'er you go.

Lydia Baxter (hymn)

I knew a Malchus once.
Severely wounded
by a Peter's sword:
crazed by anger,
dazed by pain,
he thrust aside
with awful pride
that Gentle Hand

Whose touch alone
could make him
whole again.
"Have Jesus touch me?
Hell!" he hissed,
"twas His disciple
swung the sword,
aiming for my neck
and missed;
I want no part
of Peter's Lord!"

Strong Savior Christ
so oft repelled,
for rash disciples
blamed!

Poor wounded fools,
by pride compelled
to go on living
—maimed!

Ruth Bell Graham

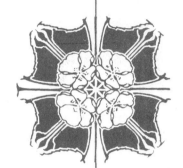

Walk boldly and wisely. . .There is a hand above that will help thee on.

Phillip James Bailey

It seems to me that we Christians have an idea here that the world is in tremendous need of. We need to say that we know the way, the way of love and peace. We will not confront the world with guns and bombs, but we will confront the world with our utter helplessness except for the strength of God.

Clarence Jordan

In our home in Haarlem, Holland, Father used to read Psalm 91 from the Bible and pray the very moment the first of January began. We consciously went into the new year together with the Lord. Do you fear the possibilities of this new year? Do as Father did. Trust and Lord that in these coming days he will be your hiding place.

Corrie ten Boom

"The bamboo for prosperity," a Japanese friend explained to me, "the pine for long life, the plum for courage—"

"Why the plum for courage?" I asked, picturing courage as a great oak.

"Yes, yes," answered my Japanese friend. "The plum for courage, because the plum puts forth blossoms while the snow is still on the ground."

Anne Morrow Lindbergh

THE TASK THAT IS GIVEN TO YOU

To each one is given a marble to carve for the wall;
A stone that is needed to heighten the beauty of all;
And only his soul has the magic to give it grace;
And only his hands have the cunning to put it in place.
Yes, the task that is given to each one, no other can do;

So the errant is waiting; it has waited through ages for you.
And now you appear; and the hushed ones are turning their
    gaze,
To see what you do with your chance in the chamber of days.

                         Edwin Markham

I am not bound to win,
But I am bound to be true.
I am not bound to succeed,
But I am bound to live up to what light I have.
I must stand with **anybody that stands right**,
Stand with him while he is right,
And part with him when he goes wrong.

                     Abraham Lincoln

    It needs courage to let our children
go, but we are trustees and stewards and
have to hand them back to life—to God.
As the old saying puts it: "What I gave
I have." We have to love them and lose
them.

                     Alfred Torrie

How firm a foundation, ye saints of the Lord,
Is laid for your faith in His excellent Word!
What more can He say than to you He hath said,
To you who for refuge to Jesus have fled?

"Fear not, I am thee;" O be not dismayed,
For I am thy God, and will still give thee aid;

I'll strengthen thee, help thee, and cause thee to stand,
Upheld by My righteous, omnipotent hand.

When through the deep waters I call thee to go,
The rivers of woe shall not thee overflow;
For I will be with thee, thy troubles to bless,
And sanctify to thee thy deepest distress.

Old hymn

I expect to pass through life but once.
If, therefore, there be any kindness I
can show, or any good thing I can do to
any fellow-being, let me do it now, and
not defer or neglect it, as I shall
not pass this way again.

William Penn

SLAVES

They are slaves who fear to speak,
   For the fallen and the weak;
They are slaves who will not choose,
   Hatred, scoffing and abuse;
Rather than in silence shrink,
   From the truth their needs must think;
They are slaves who dare not be,
   In the right with two or three.

James Russell Lowell

Trust in the Lord with all thine heart;
and lean not unto thine own understanding.
In all thy ways acknowledge Him,
and He shall direct thy paths.

Proverbs 3 :5,6

CREDITS

BENSON COMPANY, INC.: The words from "Because He Lives" by Gloria and William J. Gaither, copyright © 1971 by William J. Gaither. All rights reserved. Used by permission of the Benson Company, Inc. Nashville, TN.

CHANCEL MUSIC, INC.: "I'd Rather Have Jesus," copyright © 1967. Used by permission.

CHOSEN BOOKS: Excerpt from *The Vine Life*, copyright © 1980 by Colleen Townsend Evans; excerpt from *The Prayers of Peter Marshall*, copyright © 1954 by Catherine Marshall. Used by permission of Chosen Books, Lincoln, VA. 22078.

DAVID C. COOK PUBLISHING COMPANY, INC.: Excerpt from *Good News* is for Sharing by Leighton Ford, copyright © 1977; excerpt from *The Key to a Loving Heart* by Karen Burton Mains, copyright © 1979. Used by permission of the David C. Cook Publishing Company, Elgin, IL. 60120.

DODD, MEAD & COMPANY: Excerpts from *My Utmost for His Highest* by Oswald Chambers, copyright © 1935. Used by permission of Dodd, Mead & Company.

DOUBLEDAY & COMPANY, INC. Excerpt from *Angels: God's Secret Agents* by Billy Graham, copyright © 1975 by Billy Graham; prayer "Bring Us Together" from *I've Got To Talk to Somebody, God,* by Marjorie Holmes Mighell, copyright © 1968, 1969 by Marjorie Holmes Mighell. Used by permission of Doubleday & Company Inc.

LOUIS EVANS JR. Excerpts from *Creative Love* copyright © 1977, Louis Evans Jr. Used by permission of the author.

THE BILLY GRAHAM EVANGELISTIC ASSOCIATION: Excerpts from *Day-by-Day With Billy Graham* compiled by Joan Winmill Brown, copyright © 1976; excerpt by Ralph S. Bell, *Decision*, copyright © 1968; "The Incident in the Bus Station" by Lucille Campbell, *Decision*, copyright © 1968; excerpt by Stephen F. Olford, *Decision*, copyright © 1969. Used by permission of The Billy Graham Evangelistic Association.

HARCOURT BRACE JOVANOVICH, INC.: Excerpt from *North to the Orient* by Anne Morrow Lindbergh, copyright © 1935. Used by permission of Harcourt Brace Jovanovich, Inc.

HARPER & ROW PUBLISHERS, INC.: Excerpts from *Jesus* by Malcolm Muggeridge, copyright © 1975 by Malcolm Muggeridge; "If Death Were Not a Beginning" from Poems by John Tagliabue, copyright © 1959 by John Tagliabue; excerpts from *The Person Reborn* by Paul Tournier, copyright © 1966 by Paul Tournier. Reprinted by permission of Harper & Row Publishers, Inc.

JAN—LEE MUSIC: "Let There Be Peace On Earth" by Sy Miller & Jill Jackson, copyright © 1955. Used by permission of Jan—Lee Music.

LAUBACH LITERACY INTERNATIONAL: Excerpt from *Prayer: The Mightest Force in the World* by Frank C.

INDEX